MW01644706

Table of Contents

Please feel free to leave a review at mondareynoldsbooks1@gmail.com or on my facebook page.

Cover design by Getcovers.com

Preface

First and foremost, I want to state clearly that I am not a disgruntled employee and I hold no hatred in my heart for anyone. I write this book using real examples and occurrences; I am merely presenting the situations, not laying blame. I believe that by giving concrete examples, you the reader will more clearly understand my ideas. I have been as honest and raw as I can be. Growth only occurs through experience and reflection.I feel blessed to continue working in education and helping to mold the lives of young adults.

All my teaching and administrative experiences have been in the Missouri public school system. Here is what I believe about private schools, charter schools, and homeschooling: Any educational system is better than no educational system. Kids need to be in school.

Private schools require paid tuition, and many families cannot afford to pay for that type of education for their children; some parents struggle just to provide food for the family. Because parents must individually pay tuition for private schooling, a wide division grows between the haves and have-nots. Some private schools cost $20,000 or more per year, often higher than some universities. Private schools can select who they allow to attend their schools and who they can turn down. Because of the application process and tuition costs, private schools usually have a smaller student body than public schools; consequently, private schools have fewer discipline problems and most likely higher test scores. Private schools are certainly less inclusive. Public schools accept EVERYONE.

Charter schools, like private schools, are allowed to choose their students, often through recruitment. I believe that charter schools do try to have a more diverse group of students when compared to private schools; however they are still not as diverse as public schools. Most charter schools are in or in close proximity to larger cities. Unless parents can drive their students to and from school, or the charter school is willing to transport the students to and from school, many students are without the opportunity to attend. Again, this creates a

have-and-have-nots scenario.

Homeschooling has increased in popularity in recent years. Because of COVID-19 coupled with school bullying and school shootings, many parents have chosen to educate their children at home. There are many home school models. Some parents choose to use a one-on-one approach for their own children. Other parents have created a homeschool co-hort where several parents have joined together and they each teach a subject area. Some homeschooled students attend public schools for non-core classes such as band, music or PE. I understand that parents are scared and want to protect their children, but being in the field of education, I of course believe the best education occurs at public schools by trained teachers. Even though some homeschooled students' parents have a teacher certificate, most do not. The socialization skills that students learn while at school are also valuable world experiences that most homeschooled students don't receive in the isolation of homeschooling.

As a nation, we have spent so many years trying to put all students on a level playing field in education. It appears to me that moving students to private schools, charter schools or homeschool moves us further from this goal instead of closer. Any of these models allows for parent choice, but this is not a luxury afforded to everyone.

Introduction

In September of the 2023-2024 school year, I visited with the high school instructional coach and the district superintendent of curriculum about the many problems going on in education and the world, and it was then that I decided that I wanted to do something to make things better. We talked about how it seems change only happens when people get involved, like during the civil rights movement. More recently change occurred through the auto workers' and writer's strikes. If people are passionate about something, they must visibly and physically do something, and most people don't have or make the time to influence change. Eleanor Roosevelt once said, " It isn't enough to talk about peace. One must believe in it. And it isn't enough to believe in it. One must work at it."

Signing a petition to initiate change is no longer good enough. Former President John F. Kennedy had an inspiring quote, "One person can make a difference, and everyone should try." I knew I wanted to do something, and in September 2023 I started researching to write this book. This is my cause, my protest, and certainly my passion. Recently I watched the movie *Nyad* and instantly knew I had to write this book. This film tells the story of the great swimmer Diana Nyad, who at 61 decided to swim from Cuba to Florida, a swim that had defeated her 30 years earlier. The first five minutes of the movie felt like it was speaking only to me about how I must follow through on my passion. It also helped to solidify that I had to write this book because I am 61. Coincidence? I don't believe so. Rosa Parks, activist, said, " We fail when we fail to try."

My cousin, Vicky was one of the first to know that I planned to write a book and she read my original few pages. Vicky, her best friend Janna, and I were discussing my book when they shared their admiration for me.;they wished they had found an occupation that moves them as much as education moves me.

It truly breaks my heart to witness the decline of education in the United States. Education is what I love. Helping people and helping students learn is what I was meant to do. Other than being a parent, there is nothing I would rather do. We are creating a world where students can't read cursive, can't count change and are not prepared for the jobs needed to move our country forward. It saddens me that our country no longer values education as it once did. Through this book, if I can improve education for at least one person, I will be happy and consider this book a success; but I hope it touches many more people and causes them to think.

Meeting the Author

Who am I and what do I know? I grew up in a small town in West Central Missouri and was fortunate enough to attend kindergarten through twelfth grade in the same school district. In elementary school, Teachers always paired me with the slower learners to help them finish their work. Looking back, I guess that I was destined to be a teacher.

I played basketball and I was the manager for both volleyball and softball all four years. Other than cheerleading, those were all the sports available for girls. I was also the class president all four years of high school, mostly because no one else volunteered. On graduation night, I was to give a speech and was so nervous I thought I would pass out. My mom gave me one of her valiums to help relax me and it worked. After the ceremony, I was so tired that while others were out celebrating, I went home to bed.

Looking back, taking my mom's medication was not a smart decision. She was trying to help, but I don't advise this.

My parents were married for over four decades until my dad passed away from esophageal cancer at age 64. I lost my mom in 2021 to brain and lung cancer as she sat in her chair at my home. I had two older brothers; I say had because I have lost both my brothers as well. Gary, an alcoholic, committed suicide at age 59. My oldest brother Mark quickly lost his battle with cancer in 2023.

Even though I always felt different growing up, I didn't truly figure out why until I was in college: I am gay. I was molested as a child by a neighbor, which I did not remember until about ten years ago and my mom only found out then as well. I share these things so you can know me a little better; more importantly, because my experiences parallel the struggles of those students who teachers see each day. Teachers have become saddled daily with these and even more issues. We all have baggage. The key is learning to function each day, dealing with these issues and not allowing them to affect performance.

I was a first-generation college graduate. While in college, I was the field hockey manager until the university dropped it to save money. I also worked with the softball and volleyball teams as a manager/athletic trainer until I started student teaching, where I split half the time in physical education and the other half in special education.

I planned to major in nursing but quickly changed my mind and degree. During my freshman year of college one of my roommates was a nursing major and studied much and slept little. I knew I couldn't function on that little sleep. Consequently, in 1984 I earned a double major in physical education and special education from Central Missouri State University, (CMSU) now The University of Central Missouri (UCM), in Warrensburg, Missouri.

My first teaching position began in a self-contained EMH (Educable Mentally Handicapped) classroom of grades six through eight, at a west central Missouri middle school. The EMH classification has since changed to ID (Intellectually Disabled). Although I reviewed the goals of each student written in their IEPs (Individual Education Plan), I never looked at their IQ. I didn't want paperwork telling me what the students could or couldn't do; I wanted them to show me. Test scores can be skewed in so many ways. I wanted to meet each student where they were and help them grow from there. These students were so much fun,eager to learn, and this 21 year old was in love with the career and the students.

During my first year of teaching my principal questioned my judgment about taking my class to sit in the lunchroom with the rest of the student body. Not a great way to start my career. I had so much to learn. The teacher who had previously taught this class for many years was retiring. I soon learned that the students in my classroom had never been allowed to eat in the lunchroom with the rest of the students in the school and I'm still not sure why.

Nonetheless my para and I escorted and dined with our class and the rest of the school. Shortly thereafter my principal saw the value of combining all middle school students in the lunchroom. I also learned that my students typically were not allowed in the halls during class changes like all students. I watched as one of my boys stood in the hall during class change looking intrigued. I mentioned this to a veteran teacher, and he said, "your students were never allowed to mingle with the other students ." I felt like I had missed a memo somewhere. I was very confused, but I changed nothing and continued to allow my students a break during class change just like everyone else. Soon my students no longer stood and stared because they were no longer isolated. Now they fit in. Special Education has come a long way in thirty years but still needs to grow.

While teaching and coaching middle basketball and volleyball, I continued my education at CMSU,where I earned my master's degree in LD (learning disabilities). After eight years in the

EMH classroom, I moved to a learning disabilities classroom in the same building and stayed there for a year. I never stopped loving these students and have fond memories of making Christmas stockings, participating in the Special Olympics, learning, and laughing together. The students taught me as much as I taught them.

At the beginning of my tenth year of education, I accepted a job at a high school in a larger district considered to be a first runner in inclusion, where I taught these classes. Inclusion, a new initiative in the early '90s, placed IEP students in regular classrooms coupled with teacher support instead of isolating them in a separate setting. Today the phrase inclusion has been replaced by the term co-teaching, which can look different from building to building and district to district, based on the paired teachers' chemistry and the knowledge base of subject matter. One of the teachers I was fortunate enough to co-teach with in mathematics was Susan Seipp. Susan believes she has the "missionary spirit"for her subject. She says, " Many people are talented mathematicians but can't teach their way out of a bag. She continued stating she knew given the chance, she could convince those who would lend an ear they were capable of learning some mathematics. A good missionary in the traditional usage has a message he or she believes is worth hearing and the missionary can and wants to deliver the message to listeners. A good teacher is not much different." Susan and I were very comfortable working together and made a great team.

I also taught a few replaced/self-contained classes in science and adaptive physical education. Replaced classes are taught by a special education teacher with only special education students. I continued teaching in the replaced and co-teaching classes for nine years. During this time, I coached basketball and cheerleading. I also furthered my education by completing my Specialist Degree in Administration, grades five through twelve.

After eighteen years in the classroom, I was ready for a new challenge. My dad thought I would make a great principal, but sadly he passed before he saw me achieve our dream. As an administrator I thought it would allow me to reach more people and potentially change more lives. I had the opportunity to move into an assistant principal position at the same high school where I had been teaching . Both the superintendent and the building principal communicated that I'd have to abandon my teacher friends. This was difficult to do. I didn't necessarily abandon them but could no longer hang out with them as much. I understood the reasoning behind this and thankfully so did my friends. The district administration team, especially the high school admin team all became my friends.

Not long into my administrative role, several of the high school volleyball players arrived drunk at the Friday night football game. Many of these girls were starters on the team and I had to suspend them. Welcome to the big leagues! This part of the job was not fun. A couple of the girls had played basketball for me during their freshman year, and I felt like I knew them and their families well. I lost more than one night of sleep over this. Despite what many people may think, disciplining students is never fun.

Another time a boy at the high school was in the hall without a pass, so I escorted him back to class and explained to his teacher what had happened. He was going to receive a 30 minute detention. The rules were known by all the students, so it was no surprise. The students were required to sign the student handbook stating they had read it and agreed to the information and consequences contained within. This boy's dad marched into the school, demanded to speak to the principal, and came unglued. As we met in the principal's office he yelled at me and called me a dyke. After that comment, the principal excused me from her office. This was the first and only time I have ever been personally attacked because of who I am, and it hurt me to my core. Even though this man was upset at me, I knew I had done nothing wrong. He attacked me as a person and that is unacceptable. Since that time I have heard that the superintendent had a conversation with this parent, and he wasn't allowed back in the high school. I realized that this wasn't my problem, but this man's. To come unglued over a thirty-minute detention was not what he was upset about; he had something else going on in his life and I received the brunt of it. I learned not to take things personally. Also, I knew that fortunately I was backed by my principal and superintendent, which was very empowering.

Being an assistant principal wasn't all negative. I enjoyed rewarding students for perfect attendance and watching them excel in plays, athletics, band, and talent shows. Most of my job involved students and discipline, but also I evaluated teachers. I have been blessed to work with many great teachers and view some amazing lessons. Of course, with the good comes the bad, and I have seen some *bad* teachers.

As an administrator at the high school involves supervision of events, sometimes up to three nights a week. My oldest son had just been born. I hated being away from him and the late nights were exhausting. After seven years as an assistant principal I accepted a principal ship at an elementary school grades three through five. My second son was born during this time. Even though I chose to move positions, it was hard to leave the high school, the staff, and the students I worked with each day. Change is always hard, but growth usually doesn't occur without it.

Elementary school is different from high school. I know this sounds like a simple statement , but kids are kids no matter what age they are, and I love them all. Most of all I loved the enthusiasm of elementary students. They were so easily excited about basically anything, and they loved me unconditionally.

When I hit my thirtieth year in education, a financial advisor suggested retiring would financially be my best move. So, with a heavy heart, I retired at age 52. Speaking of change being hard, I struggled. After four days off I freaked out. I had always worked and now I didn't know what to do with myself. My next employment would be at a farm and home store, completely out of education.

Simultaneously, I was involved in a long and ugly custody battle that took my sons halfway across the state. I saw them every other weekend, but only if I drove six and one-half hours on Friday and six and one-half hours again on Sunday, over five years.

If you're keeping track…three degrees: BS, MS, and Ed Specialist; add teacher, assistant principal, principal, parent, and even a kindergarten summer school internship, makes a grand total of thirty years in multiple levels of education.

Last year, 2022-2023 and currently, 2023-2024, I'm back in the classroom full time in special education because of the teacher shortage. The district middle school and high school operate on an A&B block schedule, teaching middle school one day and high school the next. I've been back and forth so much that I believe this is at least the fourth time I have returned to teaching since retiring. I decided after thirty-four years that I know education and life well enough and may have some answers about how to make education and the world better.

The fact that I'm back teaching for the fourth time would lead one to assume education is in trouble. Your assumption would be correct, in both buildings where I teach, most days there are not enough substitutes to cover for absent teachers. More often than not classroom teachers must give up their plan period to fill the void. The district does minimally compensate them but constantly being asked to cover for someone else gets old and leaves that teacher behind in their preparation. I still love students and love teaching students, as do many retired teachers. As of the 2023-2024 school year, many schools could not have opened their doors if retired teachers had not returned to the classroom. I heard of one district in Kansas that had thirty retired teachers come back to teaching or they would not have been able to start school on time. Education is in crisis.I know that we have heard these words before. The famous Coleman report of 1966 showed Americans our dysfunctional educational system. This report outlined the alarming extent to which students from low-income minorities fell behind their more fortunate counterparts, creating a nation with two separate and radically unequal educational systems (Weber 3).Then seventeen years later, the National Commission on Excellence in Education issued its report on the declining quality of American schools. This report, titled "A Nation at Risk: The Imperative for Educational Reform,"boldly laid out "If an unfriendly foreign power had attempted to impose on America the mediocre educational performance that exists today, we would have viewed it as an act of war" (Weber 3). Thirty years after "A Nation at Risk" was released, much finger-pointing and confusion about education reform occurred.

In response to continued failing education, President George W. Bush and the late Senator Edward M. Kennedy spearheaded No Child Left Behind in 2002. Its goal was 100% proficiency in math and reading. Eight years later in 2010, the United States ranked twenty-fifth in math and twenty-first in science among 30 developed countries. As a result, The Common Core Standards initiative, a movement led by the nation's governors and state superintendents,brought together parents, teachers, principals, researchers, and other educational experts to develop consistent rigorous academic standards. Many of those who developed the Common Core knew from the beginning that there were weaknesses because the standards were not coupled with lesson plans, textbooks, and widespread teacher-training programs. Different states, different regions, and different teachers in different cultures were to teach these standards in their preferred ways. All students would be taught the same high standards, wherever they lived and no matter where they went to school. Jack Schneider, a professor of education at the University of Massachusetts- Lowell, said the idea of shared national standards made sense, but that it was naïve to expect them to make a big impact on student achievement without broader investments in early childhood education, teacher training, and school integration.

From its inception I too saw a big problem with Common Core . The standards are not necessarily taught in the same order in different districts and different states. This would not be a problem if students didn't move and switch schools. So, the outcome when a student moves often is they may be taught one standard twice or more, but miss being taught another standard altogether. This is especially hard on students in military and migrant worker families . The Common Core initiative seems that it may have been a knee-jerk reaction to try and solve the education problem, but it has not worked. It was a great idea in theory but think about it realistically. There are about 567 public school districts in Missouri alone. Each one of these districts was to teach the same standards. Now multiply that by each of the fifty states. There is no way that everyone was teaching what they were supposed to be teaching! I tend to be a glass-half-full kind of person, but I'm also realistic. I remember being at an education conference at the Lake of the Ozarks when I first became an elementary principal as they were first beginning to talk about implementing the Common Core Standards. I asked the question then about students frequently moving and what would be done to ensure that gaps weren't created. The response I received was "We are working on that."

Several states have now abandoned teaching the Common Core standards. I know that Missouri has adopted The Missouri Learning Standards. They are to provide clear, specific learning objectives for each grade level and subject area. These standards are aligned with the Show-Me Standards, which define what all Missouri high school graduates should know and be able to do. Were these paired with textbooks, lesson plans, and teacher training as they were created or were they just handed to teachers who were expected to figure it all out.

Another problem with Common Core was those who dictated what should be taught were too far removed from education if they were ever even involved in education except for attending school themselves. I believe anyone who is helping improve education should not be away from the classroom for more than five years. Amy Wilkins, a long-time advocate in Washington for racial equity in education, and currently senior vice president at the National Alliance for Public Charter Schools, says, "There is too much space between the people who cook up these policies and the classroom" (Sharrett 2020) I still believe former President Barack Obama was correct when speaking about Common Core as compared to the success other countries have educating their youth: "It is not that their kids are any smarter than ours-it's that they are smarter about how to educate their students "(Weber 2010). We must figure out the correct way to educate our students, our future. Everyone should want them to have the best possible education.

We do have groups of people across the United States who want our students to receive a great education. Unfortunately, until we get government officials, both state and federal, on board and are willing to provide the necessary funding, it will not be easy. Dr. Martin Luther King Jr. said, "We need leaders not in love with money but in love with justice. Not in love with publicity but in love with humanity." If our children are not important enough to want to do our best for them, then maybe I live in the wrong country.

What is the biggest factor in student success? Without question, it is teachers and their performance. Skilled and dedicated teachers need resources, training, rewards, and encouragement. The small number of ineffective teachers should be moved out of the classroom. Some might believe that because of the current teacher shortage; schools can't afford to dismiss ineffective teachers because they have no one to replace them. I disagree with this idea. I believe that poor teachers should be immediately removed from the classroom. I will speak more about this later.

The current curriculum has not kept pace with the world and needs to be revamped. In 2021, Dr. Howard E. Fields III wrote *How to Achieve Educational Equity*. In his book, Dr. Fields talks about inequalities that are plaguing our educational system. Dr. Fields points out that over a century ago, the education system developed skilled workers for industry and factory systems (Fields xvii). We need trained workers in other areas such as technology now. The educational system is in trouble from top to bottom. People in the United States, and the world, rally together in times of crisis. The Maui fires, 9/11, Damar Hamlin, tornadoes, and earthquakes are all examples of crises. Where is that commitment and resilience for the educational system that affects everyone worldwide? What is going to happen to education when retired teachers stop coming back to help?

In this book, I will provide parent, teacher, and administrator views on the current educational system, and what students believe needs to happen to improve education. I will share what improvements I believe need to be made at each of the levels to make education more successful and sustainable. I do believe that I touched more lives being a principal instead of a teacher. By writing this book, I truly believe that I can influence more lives than I have previously been able to.

The title of this book is, "*Improving the World Through Education One Day at a Time*." Why not? Educators are expected to do everything else, so why not change the world?

Summary

I am a parent of two young men and two male dogs, Sterling and Bronze. However, I carry thousands of students with me each day. Once you are one of my students you are always one of my students. I have been a teacher/assistant principal/principal/teacher for 34 years. I have been at every building and level of education except for first, second, and college-age students. I believe that education is the greatest profession in the world.

I started teaching in 1984 in a self-contained special education classroom at the middle school level. After eight years there I taught in a learning disabilities classroom in the same building. The following year I got a job in a neighboring district teaching high school self-contained classes, adaptive physical education, and inclusion. After 18 years as a teacher, I moved into an assistant principal role. My final transition of my first life in education was to become a principal at a three-through five building.

Education is in crisis. We have lived through The Coleman Report, A Nation at Risk, No Child Left Behind, and Common Core Initiatives; yet United States education continues to fall below expectations and below that of other countries. “It is not that our students aren’t as smart as other countries, but that other countries are smarter about teaching their students”, said former President Barack Obama.

Currently, we have a teacher shortage problem because of COVID-19, retirement, and a lack of college graduates going into education. We must develop a plan to educate our youth, so they not only survive but thrive. We need to figure out how to replace retiring teachers and encourage people to go into this great profession of education.

Historically, as a nation, problems are solved by the masses coming together. If we care about education and our youth, there is no time to waste. Today's students are our future!

Parental Perspective of Education

Because 99% of people have attended school, they believe they know "school" and everything that goes on at school. " Eighty percent of the voting public do not even have kids that attend school, but they judge us "educators" just the same, said Joe Sanfelippo, superintendent for the Fall Creek School in West-Central Wisconsin. Everyone has an opinion about what is right and more importantly, what is wrong with our educational system. All parents want their children to be successful, I am 100% convinced of this; unfortunately, without hard work from everyone, some milestones just won't happen.

Students arrive at school and, depending on how big the school is, are placed in classrooms with fifteen to thirty other students. Fifty years ago, most classes were filled with predominantly white students with a few black students, and class sizes were much smaller. Today, classes are more diverse than ever. Not every student comes with the same background information, experiences, and opportunities as the student next to them. Parents believe that no one is as smart, artistic, athletic, or cute as their child. I know, I'm a parent first and no different from any other.

Many years ago, teachers were looked upon as someone of high esteem. Parents invited the teacher to dinner and brought them baked goods. The American Dream existed. Buzz Aldrin, a former astronaut, has been quoted as saying, "I think the American Dream used to be achieving one's goals in your field of choice, and from that, all other things would follow. Now, I think the Dream has morphed into the pursuit of money: Accumulate enough of it, and the rest will follow." What happened to this American dream? Just a few more than one-third of the voters in a Wall Street Journal/NORC survey in November 2023, said that the American dream still holds, substantially fewer than the fifty-three percent who said so in 2012 (Lerer). Due to the changing economy of the 1970s, single-income households could no longer sustain a middle-class way of life and that called for women to participate more fully in the workforce. In a two parent/ adult household, both usually worked to put food on the table, leaving little time or energy to help their struggling student with homework. In a one-parent family, life was more exhausting with less time to help with schoolwork. According to a PEW Research Center study, twenty-three percent of students in the United States live with a one-parent family (2020). That is three times more than any other country in the Nation. Students who meet regular educational standards require help with homework when they are young; students below average or with an IEP need additional assistance. It should also be remembered, now with both parents working to make ends meet, that students were often coming home to empty houses and it was the beginning of "latchkey kids." Most students are not disciplined enough to come home from school and start doing their homework without supervision.

I was fortunate enough to grow up in the 60s and 70s when my mom was able to stay home and not work outside of our house. She was always there when we got home from school to ask about our day . She would quiz us on spelling words, make Valentine's Day boxes with us, and cook a family meal each night. As I grew older, she would run play lines with me or help me practice a speech. The entire time I was in school my family ate dinner together and discussed our day. These are some of the most vivid family memories I have.

Parents today who try to help students with their homework often become confused and frustrated with unfamiliar ways to solve problems. Many subjects like math and science are being taught differently. “Number bonds” is one such example that requires students to write the solutions of equations in stacked circles. This was a whole new language for parents (Sharrett 2020). Lindsey Burke, director of the Center for Education Policy at the Conservative Heritage Foundation, who fought against Common

Core, said, “that the standards had disempowered parents” (New York Times).

Parents expect, as they should, that the teachers will teach, students will learn, and everyone will get along. This is certainly not the case. Often now, if a teacher emails or calls home about a student, the parent immediately becomes defensive, often stating that their child would not have called someone a name or done poorly on an assignment. Someone else must have started it. You, the teacher, have the wrong student or are not doing your job! This conversation would have never taken place fifty years ago. If a parent was called during that time, the parent would have 100% agreed with the teacher, and the student would have been disciplined at home and would have apologized the next day at school.

Today, when the student arrives home from school after a teacher or principal has called or emailed about an alleged incident ,most but not all parents will question their child. Because parents want to believe their child, based on their child 's side of the story, parents will make their determination. Most young kids are honest, but as kids get older, they learn to manipulate or distort the truth. Kids are smart and most read the room well, knowing how to keep peace in the family. In my experience, the older the student, the more the parents tend to believe the student's account.

In fact,the biggest difference between being an elementary principal and a high school principal is the **parents**, not the students. If I called a parent of a high schooler to discuss their student's consequences, 40% of the time the parent did not believe me or cussed me out. At the elementary level, 95% of the parents trusted what I was telling them truly happened, thanked me for calling, and said they would take care of it at home. I get it! No parent or guardian wants to be "those" parents whose child can't keep up academically or is constantly in trouble. As an elementary principal, I dreaded calling home every time, especially because often I was making repeated calls to the same parents and I could hear the disappointment in their voices. I hated that for everyone. I had been in this district long enough that I was calling parents who were previously my high school students about their child; this helped break the ice and ease the conversation. After the phone call ,some parents will try to work with their students to correct poor behavior; but sadly parents grow tired of this, and patterns repeat. Parents are exhausted and need help. Most are doing the best they can just to survive.

School used to be a safe place. Now parents worry incessantly about their students while attending school: are the teachers qualified, do they have solid values, do they treat all students fairly? With so many teachers currently being arrested for sexual misconduct and improper acts with students, parents rightly have a reason to be concerned. Nearly 350 public educators were arrested in the United States in 2022 for child sex crimes. Unfortunately,these offenders give good teachers a bad name.

Until the Columbine High School shootings of 1999, never before had parents contemplated such dangers. According to the Gun Violence Archive in 2023, there have been 566 mass shootings across the country. In the United States, there have also been 30 school shootings as of October s in 2023. How sad parents now bear this stress. As a parent and a teacher, I have told my sons that this is the only time that they can be selfish.; if a shooter enters their building, I do not want them trying to be heroes.

Of course, schools are not the only places that we must worry about shootings. As I am writing this, former colleagues lost their twenty-four-year-old daughter to gun violence associated with drugs. She was murdered before as her young adult life was just starting.. A parent is always a parent and worries about their kids no matter how old they are.

Often public gatherings are riddled with violence. The Kansas City Chiefs won their third Super Bowl on February 11, 2024, and on February 14, 2024, the parade and celebration took place in

Kansas City, MO. Many schools within a seventy-mile radius were closed so teachers and students could attend the parade along with tens of thousands of others. Over 800 police personnel ran security at this event. As festivities closed gunshots rang out,one person lost their life, and 21 others sustained injuries., nine of which were children with gunshot wounds. Two juveniles and four adults have since been arrested in connection with the shootings. What was the reason for this incident? One individual stared at another for too long. Staring! Guns were fired because of a stare! If someone is crazy enough to fire shots because another is staring at them with such a heavy police presence, they are not fearful of anything. Some are questioning if the parents of these juvenile shooters might be held responsible for their child's involvement. In a recent school shooting in Michigan, both parents of the shooter have been convicted of involuntary manslaughter and each could face up to sixty years in prison. Their son received a life sentence. I believe this is a step in the right direction and will establish precedence for other parents to keep guns out of their child's hands. As I was watching the news after the ruling for the father of the Michigan student was announced, many community members asked what schools will do to stop school shootings. Schools are constantly looking for ways to stop school shootings, but this is a societal problem. The schools are not the ones providing these minors with guns, and everyone needs to be part of the solution. When will it end?

It is so sad that parents must worry about these things, but they also fret about drug use. Fentanyl is so dangerous and is killing many of our young people. According to usafacts.org in 2022, 73,654 people died of fentanyl overdoses in the United States. This has more than doubled from three years prior. Narcan, the drug used to reverse overdoses, became available over the counter in September 2023. Some schools even keep Narcan on hand in case of emergencies.

A few days ago, I ran into a former student who was working at an elementary school. We talked for a little while and then I asked about her sister. She said, "Sadly she passed away two years ago of a fentanyl overdose, and I adopted her two children." Every family is touched by some tragedy. Be kind to each other. You never know what someone else is enduring.

Research led by Oregon Health & Science University reveals adolescent cannabis abuse in the United States has increased drastically, by about 245% since 2000, as alcohol abuse among teens has steadily declined. Marijuana use is at its highest in thirty years, and teens are now more likely to use marijuana than tobacco, except for vapes, according to the American Academy of Child & Adolescent Psychiatry. In 2019, a national study showed that one in eight adolescents ages twelve to seventeen used marijuana in the past year (store.samhsa.gov). The rates of daily use increased between 2018 and 2019 among eighth and tenth-grade students.

Depression, bullying, gender identity, and mental illness issues are much more prevalent than they were even fifteen years ago. Loneliness is a big problem for all ages as making friends becomes more difficult the older we get. For students that move around often, this can be a real problem. When my sons moved back with me, I worried because they spent so much time on their electronics gaming and in isolation while reestablishing friendships. I mentioned this to a friend, who happens to be a counselor. She asked me if they were gaming with others,and they were. To help me keep things in perspective,she asked me if I'd rather they were drinking at bonfires with friends like we did when we were young, or home safe and sound. Of course, the answer is home. She said there is nothing to worry about if they communicate with others through gaming, snapchat or texting.

One of the top concerns for parents is their children under the age of 18 being bullied. This has sparked many discussions about the schools' responsibility to control bullying; as a result some parents have turned to home-schooling or chosen private schools. According to a spring 2022 survey by Pew Research of teens ages thirteen to seventeen, 53% say online harassment and online bullying are major problems (Schaeffer 2). Older teen girls are especially likely to have experienced bullying. Fewer than half of those who were bullied at school in 2019-2020 said that they notified a teacher or other adult about it. In 2021, high schoolers who are gay, lesbian, or bisexual were about twice as likely as their heterosexual counterparts to say they'd been bullied, both at school and online (Schaeffer 7). "We know that victims of bullying can experience negative impacts across all domains of their lives," said Amanda McGough, a clinical psychologist who works with teenagers and adults. McGough continues to say, "Bullying affects their mental, emotional, physical, social and academic functioning which may look like a low self-esteem, depression, isolation, physical complaints like headaches or stomach aches, or avoiding going to school." Stopbullying.gov offers resources to schools on educating students about bullying. Students learn bullying behavior from somewhere. We all need to look in the mirror and make sure we are not exhibiting bullying behaviors in front of our children.

Are they watching it on TV? If we figure this out, we may be able to stop it.

The incident of Nex Benedict being bullied at their Oklahoma school has made national headlines. Although Nex was accepted at home, they were not accepted at their Oklahoma school. "Sue Benedict, Nex's parent, tells Bevan Hurley from The Independent that the gender-fluid teenager endured more than a year of abuse simply for being who they are." The bullying started at the beginning of the 2023 school year, a few months after the Oklahoma governor signed a bill that required students in public schools to use the restroom that matched the sex listed on their birth certificate. There were no gender neutral restrooms in the school Nex attended. Then on February 7, 2024, sixteen-year-old Nex got in a fight with three older girls in the girls' bathroom at Owasso High School. Nex suffered bruises over their face and eyes, scratches on the back of their head from hitting their head on the floor when knocked to the ground. Even though Nex had been bullied, they were suspended for two weeks after the altercation. The next day Nex collapsed at home and was taken to St. Francis Pediatric Emergency Room where they were later declared dead (Hurley). People like Nicole Poindexter, an associate regional campaign director of the state's Human Rights Campaign are calling for the removal of the State superintendent of Schools who made the statement, "There's not multiple genders. There are two." Poindexter said, "We told them that rhetoric of this hate would result in body bags. I am devastated to tell you that we were right" (Fenwick 2024). Why can't we just accept everyone for who they are? As of March 13, 2024, Nex's death was ruled a suicide. What harm was Nex causing? This case will be interesting to see if the school is charged with negligence. Did they fail to protect Nex as they should have? I believe they are negligent by not providing gender neutral bathrooms. To me this is such an easy fix. Since Nex's death, the Oklahoma LGBTQ suicide prevention line has seen more than a 230% increase in calls. This increase shows the need for support in mental health services. Both students and concerned parents are calling. Parents want to know what their rights are under Title IX and what they can do to persuade schools to be more proactive against reports of bullying instead of reactive (Gamble 2024). Could Nex's parents have done more? I do believe that eyes have been opened by the incident involving Nex. Nex may help change the world and protect other students, but it is so sad that Nex had to die to become a hero.

Parents worry about everything their kids do that they aren't supposed to do and everything they don't do that they are supposed to do. Parents believe they will be judged by their children's actions, and it will be a bad reflection on them as parents. Parents should not judge themselves by the mistakes of their children. They should give teenagers room to figure things out for themselves if they are not endangering themselves or others. The best parents can do, in most cases, is to be available to guide and teach when teachable moments arise (Lawlis 182).

Early in my administrative career , I was blessed to hear author Jim Kern speak. Hearing him and then reading his book, *Build the Fort Today*, changed my life and made me a better parent. I think if you read it, it will change your life as well. In short, it talks about being present in your child's life. Don't put off things your child asks you to do with them today because tomorrow may not happen. Fostering and nurturing open lines of communication now, even if they are about nothing important, will help your child be willing to talk to you when problems arise. When my oldest son was in the eighth grade, the last day of school was an eighth grade bash. Even though he still lived across the state this was my weekend. The event ran from 6-9 pm. I tried to change weekends with his other parent because this meant that we wouldn't get home until after midnight if I allowed him to go. The other parent refused to change weekends. I was faced with telling him he couldn't attend the school event or suck it up and drive late. This was the first real time that he wanted to participate in anything related to school since he had moved from my house after the 5th grade. I chose to take him, and we would deal with the late hours . Besides, they both could sleep in the car on our way home. I have never regretted this decision. My son has also thanked me more than once. It strengthened our relationship, and he knew that nothing is more important than him.

Everyone's world was turned upside down when COVID-19 hit. In the beginning, some parents were scared to send their kids to school in fear that they would contract the virus we knew so little about. Some parents did send their kids to school even when they may have been sick because they couldn't stay home with them due to work. When the schools were forced to shut down and students had to stay home from school, parents panicked. First, they panicked because they didn't know how to manage work and their children home alone. How was their student going to learn academics, make friends, and learn socialization skills? Second, parents worried because they were assuming the role of pseudo-teachers, a position most had never done before. For possibly the first time, maybe since the first school opened in 1635, did parents place a very high value on educators.

Summary

Parents have one of the hardest and most important jobs, not for the faint of heart. Most parents do the best they can; but with both parents working to make ends and helping students with homework, becoming involved with the school is sometimes neglected. As parents do try to help, they often realize that some subjects such as math are taught quite differently creating frustrations for both the parent and the student.The American Dream seems to keep getting farther away.

Parents worry about their students using drugs and alcohol and being bullied, both in person and on social media. School shootings and shootings in general add to their concerns.

COVID-19 turned everyone's world upside down. Parents were forced to become teachers. Students' social development was negatively affected as they missed their friends and teachers.

Most importantly parents must be present in their children's lives and keep lines of communication open. Parents must also communicate with the teachers' and schools, trusting that they exist to provide students the best possible education and that they truly do care about students.

Here are just a few examples of how much teachers care about their students. During my first few years of teaching, a rough little character from California came to my room with his father who could not control him. He was small in stature but big in personality. He knew more four-letter words than I did at that point. He was so cute, and I could tell that he had had a very rough life. He wore a fake leather jacket with the collar turned up, always had his hair combed just so, and had a cocky little walk. He had some relatives in town, an older aunt and uncle, who were going to raise him.. They had purchased and were remodeling a home large enough so my student could have his own room, and he was so excited. His uncle was working on the stairs and fell, killing him. The boy was devastated and so sad. His aunt could no longer take care of him by herself; his dad did not want him and his mom wasn't in the picture. I wasn't sure what was going to happen to him. I talked to my parents about him and the situation and shared with them that I would like to take him in. My parents talked me out of it, which was the best thing in the end for everyone. Teachers care more than parents will ever know.

I have had three students who have died during the school year. One was a girl who had played basketball for me during her freshman year. Amy was a junior and died in a car accident. She was a bulldog on the court and someone you wanted on your team. She was also on the school softball team. Her funeral was held in the school gym because so many people would want to attend. Many junior girls from that freshman basketball team gathered in my room and we sat together at the funeral. It was difficult to comprehend the finality of it all. She took a piece of me with her.

The second student was a Down's syndrome boy, Matt, who was so ornery but loving. He had cancer and had fought it for a while, but never let it change who he was. He would hide from me sometimes in the gym and would just giggle. I can almost hear that laugh now. He would often say, "You're a good girl." Losing him was quite difficult. I wrote a poem for his parents that was read at his funeral.

The third student, Matthew, was a quiet young man, a freshman who had just moved into the district. He was interesting to talk with but very disorganized, which I teased him about. One weekend he had his first seizure, and it was determined he had brain cancer. I was able to visit him in the hospital before he passed. I think about him often. Everyone you meet impacts your life. Every student is special and leaves an imprint that forever changes your life.

Teacher Perspective

At the dawn of the 20th century, public education was a cornerstone of the American way of life. As millions of immigrant children arrived in the United States, public schools offered them the opportunity to participate in the American Dream (Weber 16). What has happened? American education no longer affords the dreams of a wonderful education and financial independence to all. I still love what I do, or I wouldn't be here! I believe I am still effective and can relate to students. Education has changed so much in so many ways but has stayed the same in so many ways, too.

In 1984, I began my teaching career in a self-contained classroom with Educable Mentally Handicapped students, grades six through eight. Those students I worked with came to school in their best clothes,smelling the best they could, and ready to learn to their ability levels. My class included students from all levels of socioeconomic status, all with different life experiences, and some with a lot of baggage. They were no different than students entering every classroom today. A paraprofessional assisted me with the class of twelve. The only time during the day the students went to another class was for one special: art, music, or physical education. I was tasked with teaching math, spelling, history, science, health, and reading to at least three different levels in each subject area. So I knew my starting place, I began the year by giving each student baseline tests to see where they currently were academically. This is very similar to the pre-testing that we administer today. The major difference is I had to administer my tests individually with paper and pencil and today most of these tests are taken on school-issued laptops and as a group. My tests could be scored immediately and the computerized tests today take a little longer.

I poured over the results at home and worked diligently to figure out if or how I could pair any of the students together for a specific subject. I was twenty-one years old, and these students were my life. I can honestly say that I still feel the same way today about students. One difference is it seems students are more needy than previously and the number of needy is greater. Teachers who have taught several years that are still in education feel the same way. Teachers teach because it is a calling that they feel deep in their souls. It is a passion. Sometimes today, it feels as though it is less about the subject matter and more about being a counselor or sounding board. This is one way education has changed.

In the 1950s through 1970s, I'm not sure if teachers truly taught because it was their passion or it was one job that women could do outside the home;most teachers at this time were women. I am certain that my third and fourth-grade teachers were not passionate about their jobs because they were very strict and appeared not to like kids. My third-grade teacher was a stickler for your feet being under your desk and not in the aisle. If she saw someone with their feet in the aisle, she would put on high-heeled shoes and step on that person's foot. She was a bully and just mean. That would certainly not be allowed to happen today and rightly so! We were all afraid of her. I believe she had probably been teaching too long.

While in elementary school, we would have vocabulary words each week to look up in the dictionary, memorize,and share their meaning. We had weekly spelling words, a spelling workbook, and spelling tests. We practiced our cursive writing, learned our multiplication tables, and did book reports. I will tell you that I still have a great memory today, but I'm not sure if it has anything to do with all the memorizing I did as a kid or not. Third grade was a very punishing year for me. I believe partly because I was afraid of my teacher; there was certainly no relationship established there. Secondly, I was not a great reader and was embarrassed to read aloud, which we were required to do. Lastly, I experienced death for the first time. My grandpa passed away suddenly. Even though it was my mom's dad, I witnessed my dad cry for the first time, and that was gut-wrenching to watch. For several days after my grandfather's funeral I would grow upset at school and my mom would come pick me up. I include this because as teachers, we must be aware that students have more than just school going on in their lives and we must be understanding and sympathetic toward them.Parents must communicate with the school about these outside stressors.

I remember the reading groups like it was yesterday: the blue birds, red birds, and yellow birds. All students knew which group had the best readers and which group were the lower readers. These groups were not at all good for students' self-esteem. I don't believe that in the late 1960s and early 1970s teachers and education worried about self-esteem. Perhaps they were focused on teaching academics, believing that self-esteem development occurred outside of school or at home. Thank heaven we don't make students read aloud anymore unless they volunteer. These reading groups were tracking, whether it was recognized as such or not. I don't dislike tracking and believe that we should get back to tracking. However, we need to figure out a way to discreetly group students because we do need to care about student self-esteem at school. After all, many students do not receive validation at home. I believe this may be what citizen's are referring to when they say we should teach as in years past. To educate more complete learners, many teachers today think we should go back to the basics-reading, writing, and arithmetic.

When I attended elementary school in the 60s and 70s those who did well on their assignments and finished faster than most, were asked to help struggling students; there were no self-contained ,resource, or co-teaching classes. It should be remembered that IEP's or Individualized Educational Plans did not technically exist until 1975, so peer tutors were often used whether they were called that or not.

A point that teachers agree on is when the decline of education started. It is felt that in the 70s, when many families believed that both parents needed to work outside of the home to provide food for their family, is when the partnership between school and home broke down. Parents were weary when they got home from work and didn't have time or energy to work on spelling, reading, or math with their kids. Parents had to make dinner after work ,so studying spelling was not a priority at this point but survival was. I realize as I am writing this, that this was probably the beginning of our unhealthy eating habits and perhaps the start of families not eating together and discussing their days. Thus, the beginning of the family communication breakdown.

When both parents started working, it was convenient to grab fast food for the family instead of having to prepare a meal. I believe this new dinner solution led to unhealthy eating habits. That coupled with students glued to technology created unhealthy, overweight people. According to the Food Research and Action

Center 2021, in the United States, 71.6% of adults are classified as overweight or obese.

When students become difficult, parents stop helping them learn or do homework. It is easy for parents to just expect teachers, interventionists, or counselors to spend extra time with their students when they have washed their hands of them. Many parents feel that it is 100% the school or teacher's job. Parents have admitted to saying, "I give up!I can't do it anymore!" This comment was made right in front of the student. How do you think this makes the student feel? I'll tell you: worthless and burdensome. How can we expect these students to be successful if their parents are giving up on them? The student thinks, why would a teacher care if my parents don't? A parent of a middle schooler recently shared at a parent/teacher meeting he believed his eighth-grade daughter only attended school for the social aspect and that she didn't care about academics. Whose job is it to help her realize the importance of school ? The parents! You must be a parent until your student is out of your house and then you can become their friend if you choose to.

Teachers now understand, more than ever, that students don't care how much you know until they know how much you care. Some students' home lives are so terrible that school is the safest and kindest place for them. I have witnessed many times teachers being caring and empathic to student problems.

As an assistant principal at the high school, I couldn't believe the number of students who lived on their own, or on another student's couch. Couch surfing was a better resolution than their situation at their home. There are at least two sides to every story, but it was a difficult part of the job knowing this about certain students,my heart ached for them. One young man worked late on school nights, had a difficult time getting up in the morning, and was often late for school. Per the student handbook, students were only allowed a certain number of tardies per semester before discipline was to occur. After the student exceeded his number of tardies he shared with me that he didn't have an alarm, so I started calling him every morning to wake him up. It worked most of the time. Probably two years ago I ran into him at a restaurant with his wife and kids, and he said, "I want to thank you for believing I was worth enough for you to take your time to wake me up." He explained that life was good, and he was doing well. Rewarding is an understatement of how I felt when he shared his story with me. It had nothing to do with me helping him but that he has a good life now when it wasn't always the case. It is gratifying to see former students and how they have grown into successful adults.

COVID-19 was extremely hard on parents, students, and teachers and had a lasting impact on education in the United States. When everything shut down and went remote, students fell behind. As a result, the learning these students lost will need to be recouped to avoid the ripple effect down the line. Tom Kane, Faculty Director of the Center of Education Policy Research at Harvard University, 2023, said that "there is evidence that districts that spent more time shut down, in remote learning, or were in communities that saw high COVID-19 death rates, saw more learning loss than others." Making up for the learning loss requires additional instructional time, which can come in the form of a longer school year, year-round schooling, or the implementation of academic programming into summer. One advantage of extending the school year is that teachers are already in place, buildings are available, and families have the drop-off and pick-up routines down. Kane said, "We can't let this whole generation of students have a permanent decline in their post-secondary education that is going to hurt our economy and those students' future for decades to come.

Emily Erisman, M. Ed,LPC had this to share about COVID-19 when we spoke in May 2024. "The most notable differences in our incoming kindergarteners post-COVID are the significant delays they're presenting with social/emotional skills. Across the board, all students at the elementary level felt the ripple effects of losing nearly a year of social interaction with their peers due to social distancing and isolation requirements. But the largest overall effect we've seen are these students, who would've been toddlers during the COVID lockdown, struggle more than any other incoming class to date with impulsiveness, emotional regulation and overall school engagement."

A report published February 1, 2024, by the Center for Education Policy Research at Harvard University and The Educational Opportunity Project at Stanford University studied testing between spring 2022 and spring 2023, post COVID, for school districts in 30 states. The researchers found students managed to recover about one-third of the original loss in math and one-quarter in reading. The report's authors vocalize that districts need at least another year of recovery in math and two more years in reading for students to regain pre-pandemic achievement levels (Kekatos 2024).

A few years ago , a troubling trend began to spread in the United States educational system; students not showing up for school. Initially, this made sense after schools reopened after COVID-19, because many believed it would take time to reestablish daily routines. Before the pandemic about 15% of U.S. students were chronically absent from school, but as of last year it is still at 26%, which is surprising. Several specialists in the educational field offer these issues as part of the problem; illness, mental health, and transportation issues as part of the reason for this new trend. Teacher absences are also higher because more people are actually staying home when they are sick. United States students are nowhere close to making up for learning losses from the pandemic. Students who are behind academically may resist going to school which sets them back even further (Mervosh 2024).

When schools shut down for COVID-19, another problem was created for those students who were accustomed to at least two nutritional meals a day. Now, they didn't receive those meals unless they had transportation to them. Some school districts still made food available to those with the greatest need. When COVID-19 hit the United States in the spring of 2020, the USDA set up the Pandemic EBT program. This program provided eligible families with funds to purchase food to replace the meals their students would have received at school. The EBT program continued over the summer, ending in the summer of 2023. As of January 2024, the government announced that the summer EBT program will return for summer 2024 for those states participating. All students who receive free or reduced lunch through school qualify for this initiative. Nebraska and Iowa are among states not participating in the program. The governor of Iowa, Kim Reynolds, said in a statement, “An EBT card does nothing to promote nutrition at a time when childhood obesity has become an epidemic” (Luhby 1-3). I agree students should be fed nutritional food, but in these times of food insecurity any food is better than no food. Some of the problems lie in the fact that nutritional food is more expensive than non-nutritional food, so the parents try to stretch the money as far as possible. We must solve the problem of how to make nutritional foods more affordable. I am very happy and encouraged that the federal and local governments have seen the need for nutritional food year-round. Much more needs to be done about the price of nutritional food.

Schools can play a large part in helping families become more independent when it comes to food. Some schools have programs, usually taught by volunteers, that teach students the value of nutritional fruits and vegetables. These programs teach the students how to grow these items in an outdoor classroom, show the students how to prepare the food, and do taste tests with them. Minimal space is needed to implement gardens such as these. The hope is that these programs will provide the students with the tools needed to make informed decisions about foods and create more confident individuals in food choices that will carry into adulthood. Perhaps education in this area could be extended to parents. What if parents were invited to an evening event where the students teach their parents about gardening and healthy eating.

Food was not the only challenge facing students and teachers during COVID-19. The loss of connection with their peers left many in depression. Youth suicide attempts soared during the pandemic, especially among girls. Everyone had their world turned upside down and many had a difficult time adjusting, especially those not yet mature enough to rationalize and navigate through their new normal.

Good teachers don't teach subjects, they teach students/individuals. Teachers were no exception to the struggles during COVID.-19. When school closed, teachers were forced to deliver information in new and creative ways. Consequently, they taught and assigned lessons to faceless students. Some students did not receive the face to face instruction they needed and the nurturing they craved. Subjects were taught and not students. Teachers were lost, too. By nature, most teachers are social creatures. They missed their students and missed experiencing light bulbs going on in students' minds. They worried about little "Joey", who even with two teachers assisting him still struggled with his comprehension in multiple subjects. Teachers worried about all those students who previously "checked-in" daily either with them, a counselor, or a social worker, to keep their lives in balance.

Teachers also worried about each other, friends were getting sick, and some were dying alone. More than ever teachers were expected to educate students and simultaneously fight for their lives against a terrible virus. As schools reopened after COVID-19, most students returned but many educators didn't. The return after COVID-19 was by no means normal, everyone seemed on edge and angrier, almost as if those who were a little stressed before were totally on edge now.

A portion of my current job at the high school involves taking students who have IEPs out into our community to learn job skills while working at various businesses. We drive a school van with visible lettering on the side indicating the school's name. As I dropped off students to work at the local grocery store a lady stuck her tongue out at me as we were pulling into the parking lot. I have no explanation as to why she would have done this, but perhaps the stress of COVID -19 and world changes had gotten to her as well.

Teachers feel overwhelmed by the students in their classrooms who come with 504 and IEP accommodations. Regular education teachers have very limited education on how to administer these accommodations and modifications. Many colleges only require teachers to take one class focused on IEPs. Teachers are expected to implement modifications or accommodations for the numerous students in their classes based on a single piece of paper . Teachers need help to understand these accommodations and modifications. Regular education teachers need time to collaborate with the special education teachers. They are responsible for ensuring the IEP is followed and providing updates to the parents on the progress of each student. At times, this task feels unsurmountable.

Teachers need administrative support in other areas as well. They believe administrators often hide their heads in the sand about errant student classroom and building behavior. The perception is administrators remain in their office, not roaming the building supporting teachers and corralling unruly students.

Student behavior at school has changed as well since COVID-19. I am aware that there have always been fights in schools. In my thirty-four years in public schools, I have never seen as many fights happening as are occurring now. Most of them are over simple little things. These two examples, the woman sticking her tongue out at my students and me and more school fights, help to illustrate how COVID-19 has affected society more than just our health. Of course all of this cannot be blamed on COVID-19. Americans have lost their filter and ability to control their temper. Look at how grown men in Congress act, calling each other names and fighting each other over issues on which they don't agree. When did this become acceptable? It isn't!

I was involved in one altercation as a high schooler and can only remember a handful of fights during my high school years. Fights just didn't happen as frequently as they do now, at least not at school. One girl in my class, who was probably autistic, even though that wasn't a word many knew at the time, was being bullied and picked on in physical education class during a tennis unit. She had finally reached her limit and hit the bullying her with a tennis racket. The teacher didn't see this. Another person in our class was going to attack this autistic girl. I intervened and eventually held the attacker in the corner until someone got the teacher. Again, other than this incident, I can count on one hand the number of fights that occurred at the school I attended.

Another area that frustrates teachers is testing, testing, and more testing. Teachers and students alike grow weary of the endless testing that must take place over the course of the year.

There are tests in the fall, tests in the winter, and then even more tests in the spring. Some are taken in one setting while others are taken over several days; some are just for reading, some are just math, and some cover all core subjects. Much academic time is lost to administer these tests. There are state tests and national tests and I'm confident the analysis of the results are not used for improvement due to time constraints. Is one day of testing an accurate measure of a student's true ability? I believe not! Most teachers and students are tired of these state mandated tests that all seem to measure reading, even though they are supposed to assess knowledge in other subject matters. In addition to these tests, individual teachers administer formative and summative tests in the classroom.

And so, COVID-19, gun violence, drugs, lack of support physically from the school district and from parents/guardians, lack of resources for teachers, and non-stop testing have created the perfect storm that is a lack of good teachers.

Summary

Teachers are amazing people, and most of them understand the hardships students face daily. Good teachers understand that students don't care how much you know until they know how much you care.

Students who come to school are more diverse than ever before, and teachers must learn to adjust their presentation and teaching styles to match that of their learners.

Parents must communicate with the schools so teachers can recognize a student in crisis and act appropriately to help the student.

COVID-19 was difficult for everyone. People seemed more stressed during that time and continue to be. The pandemic brought out the worst in many people and the best in others. Students gained weight as they were very sedentary while on their technology. Also, since nutritious food is more expensive students were eating junk, if they had food at all. Teaching families to grow nutritional food could help some in this area. Many people lost their lives while alone and others were hospitalized for quite some time. Several teachers decided to retire or go into another field. Those intending to become teachers decided to go into another profession. Teachers had to learn to teach differently without having students in person.

Teachers today also must deal with guns in schools. They do not feel appreciated enough or get paid enough for the job they are expected to do.

Administrator Perspective

To be a good administrator you must exhibit the following: a passion for education and people, the courage to confront, the ability to be transparent, the ability to ask for help, as well as be gracious, confident, and compassionate. It is not an easy job and is often thankless. You often don't hear if you are doing things right, but certainly hear if people believe you are making mistakes.

Everyone expects district-level and building-level administrators to possess all the answers to the educational crisis. It should be no surprise, they don't. They certainly want to, but it is no easy fix. Superintendents and assistant superintendents often commit to learning initiatives that look good on paper but rarely take the time or make the time to research these new initiatives thoroughly. District-level administrators buy into an initiative and then mandate it to building administrators who are then tasked with selling this new initiative to their teachers without throwing the central office under the bus. Veteran teachers who have been around awhile, have seen new techniques, initiatives, and strategies come and go, and the same can be said for the number of superintendents.

As a principal, you feel as if you have a little more control of your building and your teachers. With more "control," comes more responsibility and more people to answer to. You receive directives from the central office as to what to implement at your building. You, the building administrator, must convincingly sell it to your staff. CO wants data and great results. You ask your teachers for data showing positive results. The teachers feel stressed and pressured to produce great results from these latest new initiatives they have been forced to implement. They may or may not have had training on these new initiatives. You as the principal feel pressure to produce positive results for the central office. You know most of your teachers are doing the best that they can, but it is not good enough. It is never good enough. There is never enough time, and you can never make everyone happy.

As a superintendent, you answer to the board of education although most believe you answer to all, and everyone wants to bend your ear. Being a superintendent in a small district looks so much different than being one in a mid-sized to large district. Some superintendents in small districts drive school buses, while managing the budget, curriculum, special services, and personnel. In larger districts, the superintendent usually has assistants to handle these departments and it is paramount they be competent . To assure your district avoids lawsuits, you must be confident your director of special services knows the law forward and backward and is up- to- date on the ever changing special education laws. This area in any district is the most vulnerable area for potential problems to occur. Once you have these people in place you must trust them and allow them to do their jobs.

The life of an assistant principal varies from building size and grade level. Often the life of an assistant principal deals with discipline, and this can be a very lonely position; but as I mentioned earlier, I watched students excel in athletics and the arts, and I awarded prizes for perfect attendance. I also evaluated teachers as I loved visiting classrooms and watching great teachers do great things. When a great teacher is on, it is like watching a professional baseball pitcher deliver a no-hitter, or a golfer hitting a hole in one; it is truly a thing of beauty! Teachers recognize when they are good, too. I remember when I was still teaching, at the end of many days I thought I was super effective and felt great about my day's work. The students seemed to grasp the concept I was teaching. On the other hand, there were days that I felt I missed the mark and that I didn't feel so good. Reteaching had to occur the next day until all students understood.

Going into a classroom where the teacher is not a great teacher is obvious from the minute you walk into the room.

Students are not engaged, and the teacher is often unorganized and rattled when you enter the room. The follow-up conference is not fun for anyone. Sometimes job targets must be written for improvement in areas of weakness. If after several attempts for improvement and the teacher still falls flat, the process of dismissal begins. This process needs to be shared with the personnel director so they are not blindsided if contacted about the situation.

I believe dismissal of a poor teacher doesn't occur often enough, especially after multiple observations in the classroom and given many opportunities for growth. Believe it or not, I have been in a classroom before when the teacher didn't even realize that I was in the room. I have been a part of four teacher terminations, all were very different situations ranging from inappropriate sexual activity with a student to just a total lack of classroom control. They were all difficult because you are affecting someone's life and their livelihood, but you must remain focused on the goal, the students. As an assistant principal, you are often the go-between the teachers and the principal. It can feel like you are teetering on a piece of playground equipment, and it is a little awkward.

Principals often become irritated with teachers for not dealing with issues within their classrooms that they sometimes create. Teachers often set classroom expectations in their classroom, which they should, but then they do not hold students accountable once they violate these expectations. This lowers the teacher's credibility as a disciplinarian and is hard to regain; this is about the worst thing that you can do to yourself. This leads to frustration for the teacher and potentially a discipline referral for the student. This could have all been avoided by the teacher following their own rules. If teachers are not going to follow their established rules, they shouldn't have them. Please don't misunderstand; if a student needs a discipline referral, please send one. My point is, do not create the problem yourself.

Teachers also frustrate their administration by wanting to collaborate, which is a great practice and is strongly encouraged.

The problem arises when some of the teachers who are supposed to be collaborating are not contributing to the conversations or pulling their weight. This teacher is wasting everyone's time. This is frustrating for administrators because often they don't find out about these "slackers "until they have been employed for years. Administrators need teachers to share both the good and the bad about their teams. There are so many more teachers in their buildings than administrators. Observing inappropriate or worrisome habits or traits is much easier for a teacher to see than for an administrator. Teachers should share this information with their administrator. In this example, the teacher is not even being asked to personally confront this person but just make the administration aware of them. How can we expect students to tell us what they have seen or heard when investigating an incident if teachers won't do the same? I do understand a little of the hesitation about reporting another colleague to the administrator because they essentially hold all teachers' careers in their hands.

Principals are not successful if the teachers in their buildings aren't successful. Principals are only human and want the best for students and teachers alike. A building principal becomes overprotective of their teachers almost like parents are with their children. None of us can operate as an island. You must trust your principal and know they are certainly discreet and would never use your name when discussing issues with your colleague, just as a teacher would never use a student's name when talking to another parent about classroom issues. Approach your principal and ask to have a conversation with them. If they are not approachable there is a problem with them, not you. Most principals are very open to any conversations that you may request to have with them. Be honest with them about what is bothering you. If it concerns you, it is important enough to discuss with them. I will guarantee you that your principal will respect you more after the conversation than they did previously. Education is a relationship business and we are all in this together: the better all of us communicate with each other the better it will be for all parties.

Another frustration for administrators is when teachers bring problems to them and deny every suggestion being offered before even trying them. Occasionally teachers just want to complain and need to be heard. So, a principal needs to be a sounding board at times and that's ok but can still be frustrating.

When I was an elementary principal, there was friction in one of the grade levels . I allowed it to go on for a while hoping for a peaceful resolution. When it became obvious that the situation was not going to resolve itself and it was affecting team cohesiveness and trickling down to the students, I stepped in. I called two of the teachers into my office. The situation was the team having conflict with just one teacher. I listened as they talked and finally said, "You can either figure this out or I will figure it out for you, but if I'm the one to resolve this, there will be paperwork involved." This meant I would write job targets. They decided that they could work it out after all. The single teacher disagreeing with the rest of the team was probably one of the best, if not the best, teachers in my building; but she was not playing nicely with the team. I kept her back after the three of us had met and I said, " if things don't change one of us is not going to be around at the end of the year, and I'm not planning on going anywhere!" I remember I immediately called another administrator and shared with them that I had just called out my best teacher. I asked them if I was an idiot for doing this? They assured me that I had done what I had to do. I hated having this conversation, but it was necessary.

I've always believed jealousy exists between elementary and secondary teachers. Because they truly don't know what the other level does, and, if we don't know something, we naturally form our own opinion. Everyone wants things to be fair and equal but they are very different, so that will never be the case. Teachers chose the level of education that they wanted to work with and should have known the trade-offs associated with each level. Currently our high releases at 2:35 ;all the students leave the classrooms and the teacher's responsibility is mostly over. The middle school gets out at 2:35 as well, bus riders are held in classrooms until all buses are dismissed, usually lasting until about 2:55. Middle school teachers supervise their students between fifteen and twenty minutes longer each day. Secondary teachers are strongly encouraged to attend their students' extra-curricular activities, but elementary teachers don't have these events to attend. Elementary teachers have playground duties in all-weather elements, but secondary staff don't have these duties. It will never be equal, but there are trade-offs at each level.

Until I was the summer school principal at the kindergarten building, I never before realized what elementary teachers did; they are amazing. They teach students how to line up, raise their hands, open their milk, count, learn their colors, add, read, and so much more. Often I'm reminded of the poster that states, "Everything I need to know I learned in kindergarten," which I think is spot on.

Secondary teachers tweak and extend what students know; they teach students how to cook, write speeches, the Pythagorean theorem, anatomy, physics, Spanish and so much more. Again, I have had a unique experience and the ability to observe and be in awe at all levels. I have shared with three superintendents how important I believe it is for each level to observe what the other level does. I suggested that in the spring after testing is completed, elementary and secondary teachers switch buildings for a day. Not all at once of course, but several at a time. It is easier to understand someone else's job when you walk in their shoes. I think this would be an eye-opening experience and both groups of teachers would gain respect for each other, eliminating envy and making a district more cohesive. Incidentally, none of the superintendents I mentioned this to ever acted on it. I still believe It has value and merit in a district.

As a principal, you also feel like you must answer to parents and teachers. It seems like you have bosses above you and below you. You want parents to step and do their job instead of trying to tell you how to do yours. Parents often refer to schools as babysitters. If teachers were babysitters, they would probably be making more money than they currently do. If teaching is so easy, parents need to become school substitutes. Passing judgment is easy looking from the outside in. Parents do not tell doctors how to do their jobs, yet they believe it to be okay to tell educators.

Another trait of a great principal is that you are constantly on high alert, looking around for potential dangerous problems. Your eyes and ears must always be open. I can't tell you how many times while just walking through the halls in the morning before school or during the passing period, I overheard information about a potential altercation or something about drugs. It is much easier to foil the activity before it happens than trying to clean up the mess afterward. If you see a principal who is relaxed during a school day, they are not doing their job correctly, or they are a very good actor. The life of a principal is stressful. Now that I am a teacher again, it is difficult for me not to be in that principal mode.

Have we done enough to keep everyone safe? Are we trained and prepared in all situations? How do we know which direction to take our district? What company or product do we believe offers the best bang for our buck in preparing students and affecting student achievement? Are teachers, paraprofessionals, and administrators I have in place, the right person for the job? Is the state going to allot us funding for the new initiative? How will I recruit and retain great teachers? None of the answers to these questions, if there are answers, can be quick. Things must be taken to the board of education for approval, or passed up the chain of command first and then taken to the board . This is very much like how the United States government works and why at times, nothing ever seems to get completed. There are many more questions than answers.

Summary

Being an administrator at any level in a school district is a tough and sometimes thankless job. Administrators have so many things to always worry about; do I have the appropriate safety procedures in place, and do I have the right teachers in the correct positions?

How am I going to convince teachers to abandon their current way of teaching and adopt the new program that the central office has just purchased, and accept that the training will cut into their summer break?

Administrators must evaluate teachers and pray they are performing well. If teachers are doing a great job, it makes an administrator's job easy. If they are not doing a good job, it involves paperwork and trying to save this teacher's career by bringing in instructional leaders or master teachers to work with them. If the struggling teacher can make some positive changes, that is a win-win situation. If the teacher cannot make important changes, then dismissal proceedings start.

Students' Perspectives and Thoughts on Improvements

Too often when we talk about fixing broken school systems, we focus on what adults think. If education is about students, we should let the students have a voice. Most of the student comments outlined here occurred after 80% of this book was complete. The impromptu conversations took place with several small groups of less than fifteen students grades 7-12. I felt the students were very reflective and honest.

A couple of the things that came from these conversations surprised me.First, the middle school students, who have not been allowed to have their cell phones during the day for the past two years, did not mention that as something they wished to change. This was encouraging because the students realized that they could survive without their phones while at school. Next, students perceived some of the same issues as problems that I perceived to be problems. This validated for me that I do still have my thumb on the pulse of education.

I simply started the conversation by saying, “Up until now in your education what do you believe has been good and what do you think would make things better?”

These comments and suggestions are taken from discussions with student groups grades seven to twelve.

1) Longer lunches- Students expressed they need more than 22 minutes for lunch.
2) Later start time for middle school and high school students- In my current district, middle and high school starts at 7:35. Elementary schools start at 8:20.
3) More activity in classes, allowing students to move.
4) More elective classes need to be available at earlier grades.

5) More flexibility from teachers of those students involved in extracurricular activities.They often don't get home until late and might complete their homework.
6) Teachers need to care more about the students' understanding of the information presented rather than just teaching the subject content; teach the students.
7) Don't force students to take classes that they are not interested in, like art.
8) Have more classes that teach life skills, like building trades and personal finance.
9) More personalization of classes at earlier grades, like computer technology, computer repair, and building trades.
10) Require only basic math and language arts classes unless students are college-bound, and then advanced classes could be required.

11) Require only basic science unless students are going into a career that requires science like health occupations or engineering, etc.
12) Classes in entrepreneurship should be taught by someone who has been a successful businessperson. Professionals who have been in the trenches have more credibility, at least in the eyes of the students. Offer classes that teach life skills, such as cooking, basic sewing, changing a flat tire, and wise consumer skills.
13) Make connections with students so they aren't afraid to ask questions if they don't understand something.
14) Stop teaching only to average academic level students. This doesn't address the needs of lower academic or the higher academic students.
15) Teach students to the point of mastery not to a specified time on the calendar that teachers want the unit to be completed. Change the teaching style if necessary.
16) Make lessons engaging.

17) Teach what students need to survive in the world, and if they are not going to college let graduate school earlier.
18) See students as real people, not just objects.
19) Find out how the students in your classes learn best and tailor learning to those different styles.

I will briefly comment on the above students' perceptions and offer any clarification needed, along with some of my own thoughts.

1. There has been real progress by making school lunches healthier and offering a greater variety of choices for students. If our goal is to teach healthy eating habits we should allow more time for students to eat. We all know it is not healthy for anyone to cram down food in 22 minutes.
2. Evidence for years has stressed that teenagers in school should have a later start time than their elementary counterparts. Research on this topic

will be discussed further in the book. If we truly want to gauge what our students know and their capabilities, we need to follow all best practices; a later start time for middle and high school students is one of those best practices.

3. Classes must be engaging. Students now are in the digital age where everything offers immediate feedback and motion is constant. Be it right or wrong, teachers must keep honing our teaching skills to keep everyone engaged.
4. If we want students to find something they are passionate about, we must start providing opportunities for them to explore careers before their junior year of high school.
5. I believe most educators do accommodate students who are involved in extracurricular activities. Oftentimes these students are more

conscientious and tend to perform better in classes.

6. Teachers must know their students. They must check often for comprehension and reteach as many times as necessary until all students understand the concept.
7. I understand that sometimes adolescents don't know what they like and don't like. Originally, the middle school concept was designed to expose students to a variety of classes and help them determine what spiked their interest; however, I believe today's students are more mature and more focused. They don't need the forced exposure to topics they already know they are not interested in.
8. For whatever reason many parents don't teach life skills to their children as much as they used to. Students are missing out on learning

important life skills, such as changing flat tires, checking the oil in vehicles, knowing what to do if an engine light comes on, washing clothes, doing laundry, and balancing a checkbook. I know not all people have checkbooks, but everyone still must know how much money they have in their accounts. These and so many other skills students are asking for but not being taught. If students are asking for them shouldn't we provide them? We used to.

9. There should be more classes offered at an earlier age specifically geared toward student interest. Non college-bound students need not take as many math, science, social studies, and language arts classes, freeing them up to take more classes of interest.

10-12. Schools should reach out to the community and

businesspeople who have been in the trenches and let them teach some classes. If a student or students want to be an author, find an author in the community to teach them, at least a few hours a week. Maybe a student eventually wants to own their own business; invite a business owner to come talk shop to the students. The same would apply to sales or automotive technologies and many others.

13. Every teacher must develop a relationship with students and get to know how they learn best. If students think you care about them, they will work much harder for you and won't feel intimidated to ask questions.

14. We must get back to tracking more, placing academically alike students together. Currently many teachers teach to the academic middle students.

This only works for one-third of the students.

15. Often teachers cannot use the same teaching style year after year because their classroom population changes; teachers must adjust to their students.

For example, a coach has different athletes each year and must tailor plays to fit those players, not make them run plays from previous years.

The rest of the students' points have been addressed in other numbered points.

After listening to their concerns, I believe these students have hit the nail on the head. They are laying out this path that we must take to make education better. We need to seriously consider their ideas.

> I saw this post on Facebook the other day and wish I could share this with every teenager. Raising Teenagers Today, "Dear Teenagers…A Harvard study found that 99% of your success depends on ONE thing: Who you associate with. You may not realize it, but you're like a chameleon. You can and will absorb the attitudes, opinions, and behaviors of those you choose to spend the most time with. If you spend time with winners and positive thinkers, you'll start to become like them. Spend time with negative underachievers, and you'll become like them."
>
> <u>Please Choose Your Friends Wisely!</u>

Summary

Students want to be seen as individuals and taught as such. We all have different learning styles and teachers must figure out what those are and tailor lessons to students' strengths.

Teachers need to develop relationships with their students so they feel comfortable asking questions and admitting they don't understand the material presented. Students want teachers to take the time to reteach material if necessary or change their teaching style to achieve mastery. Students need teachers to see them as people and teach them, the student, not just the lesson.

Students feel more elective classes offered, more engaging lessons, classes that teach life skills, and they should not be forced to take classes in which they have no interest.

Students who are not college bound question why they must stay in school after they have mastered basic skills. They also believe students with similar test scores should be grouped according to learning levels. If not, only those with average scores benefit and those with below-average or above-average scores don't advance.

Students want and need more time to eat.

Students have presented ideas that they believe will make our schools better. Their suggestions merit strong consideration.I think we should consider their suggestions.

Consideration for Parents

Parenting is and has always been a demanding but rewarding job. Being a parent of a teenager is at times almost impossible. Adolescence is a monumental phase of life, full of promise and danger. Teens are just beginning to determine how they will fit into society and what their value will be. It is never an easy period for teenagers or their parents (Lawlis 181). As students get into middle school and beyond, their friends are the biggest influences in their lives. Don't think you are a failure if you have difficulty with your child because every teenager bucks the system at some point. It is all part of growing up (Lawlis 184).

Teenagers' attitudes shift due to hormonal and brain changes. Friends have newfound influence. So it is important to take the time to get to know their friends. Parents must be present and set boundaries. (Lawlis 151), emphasizes that in adolescent and teen years, teens don't have a clue how to behave without your guidance. Do not shower them with money to go have a good time;

spend real time with them, even if it is forced bonding. Be honest with your kids if they ask you questions about when you were a kid. There is no better way to show our children how to be honest and how important that is. The six and a half hour drive to and from St. Louis every other weekend when my kids lived there was tiring but we had some best conversations during those trips. Most parents want their children to have a better life than they did; but they will not understand responsibility and the value of work if you just give them everything they want. Children change during adolescence and so should your parenting. Teens may try to push you away. Don't let them. In some ways, your child needs you more now than ever, even if they don't recognize this.

Many of the normal parental frustrations that arise during a child's teenage years stem from natural and necessary changes inside the maturing teenage brain. Your teenager's ability to gauge risks, weigh the consequences of actions, control impulses, and think long-term are all affected by a teenage brain that is rewiring-breaking old connections and making new ones (Lawlis 20).

Teenagers are vulnerable because the brain essentially rewires itself during adolescence. Many hormones flood their brain, essentially overhauling it. Near the age fourteen for girls and sixteen for boys, the brain matures with more distinctive mental and physical skill sets. For about two to nine years there is a major reduction of reasoning in two areas: loss of empathy and future ramifications of present behavior. The loss of empathy in adolescents whose brains are rewiring results in self-absorption and self-centeredness (Lawlis 68). Take the time to talk to your children about changes in their brain. They may not act like they are listening, but they are picking it up.

As Dr. Frank Lawlis talks about in his book, *Not My Child: A Progressive and Proactive Approach for Healing Addicted Teenagers and Their Families* (68) lack of judgment and self-absorption can cause a teenager to engage in irresponsible sexual behavior, and to experiment with drugs and alcohol. Sexuality seems to be much more fluid these days and at an earlier age. Because being non-binary, gay, bisexual, or pansexual is slightly more accepted today by the heterosexual world, students seem to be exploring their sexuality at an earlier age and more freely, like their heterosexual counterparts. Had other types of sexuality been as freely accepted as heterosexuality was when I was younger, I may have figured out before college that I was gay. Teens are so much more open about expressing their individuality and testing the waters earlier than years ago, feeling more free to experiment with their sexuality. I have a student at high school who prefers to be referred to as " they" or" them" and is very vocal about being called this. I try so hard to remember this because they physically look like a male; my old brain forgets sometimes because this is a relatively new term for me. Each time I use the wrong pronoun I feel terrible and must explain that I am still trying to retrain my brain, not being disrespectful. They say their parents do not accept this and still refer to them as he. I hate this for them, because I know the feeling of not being accepted for who you are can be very isolating.

I have seen many students at both middle and high school levels who struggle with their sexuality. Now, I wish I dared to speak to them and assured them that they will figure it out and all will be okay. It is such a slippery slope because some parents won't acknowledge the struggles their child is experiencing; and naturally it is scary for the child because they fear their parents will not accept their authentic self and perhaps even kick them out of their house. I would never want to get in the middle of a parent and their child, but I sure wished I would have had someone to talk to when I was younger. Until I was in my thirties, I didn't feel brave enough to share with my mom that I was gay. It was the same day that my dad was diagnosed with cancer, so I never got to tell him. My mom said that she and my dad had suspected that I was gay. I wish they would have approached me, but I guess, like me, they didn't know what to say. So, please parents, you might not always like what your child does, but you must always love them.I realize that loving your children as a teenager is sometimes much harder than loving them when they were younger.

As students age their problems continue to grow whether it be academically or behaviorally. The older students are, the less help they want to accept from anyone. However, most teenagers are seeking answers to their problems, either consciously or subconsciously. For that reason, parents must keep open lines of communication and remain actively engaged in monitoring their children's behavior during these critical teenage years when young people are so vulnerable due to their still-developing brains. It is a challenge because teenagers tend to think parents are clueless and typically reject their advice (Lawlis 30). There is such a fine line between being involved and supportive of your child and becoming a helicopter parent. Domineering parents can rob teenagers of their identity and self-determination. These teenagers may never develop self-discipline, good judgment, or their own interests because they grow up dependent on their parents to make their decisions for them.

Parents who do try to help their students with homework become frustrated because things are being taught differently than when they were in school, particularly in the area of mathematics. If teachers expect parents to help students with their homework, perhaps they could send home step by step instructions for parents, or maybe hold a brief meeting at the beginning of school to teach parents how to do the new math. I know my son used to get irritated at me because I could get the answer but he would say, "that's not right." I must admit I would get irritated too because I knew I was right. I simply wasn't doing it the way he was currently being taught.

Far too many parents accept prescription drugs to control their child's behavioral problems; it seems a faster and easier solution to drug a child than for the parent to develop the necessary parenting skills or to seek professional counseling for the child. Child psychologists are concerned that children today have fewer outlets for creativity and high energy; they are less physically active and spend more time engaged in sedentary activities, such as playing video games, surfing the internet, and watching videos or television. They believe such children aren't learning socialization skills or how to manage their own emotions and impulses (Lawlis 26). I am in no way saying that some students are not helped by medication, but I believe that should be a last resort, not the first or final answer.

I do understand that medication is necessary sometimes. One of my sons was very angry when he was forced to move away from me,and he saw a counselor for a while. He was also on medication for ADD for a brief period. Now that my son is in a stable environment, he no longer must attend counseling or take medication and is thriving. I'm very proud of the man he is becoming.

Remember the statistics on drug use earlier in the book and how marijuana use is at an all-time high, no pun intended. As of the writing of this book, cannabis possession for adults 21 and over is legal in many states. Experimentation with drugs and alcohol has been around for many years. Many adults experimented with drugs or alcohol when they were younger, the same way as teenagers do today . Now as adults looking back on some of the things we did when we were younger, we feel lucky to be alive. Our parents must have done something right since most of us are now productive citizens. Don't panic if your teenager experiments with drugs or alcohol; it is part of growing up. Talk to them about the importance of maintaining trust and moral values, being conscious of physical safety, and understanding the dangers of drug and alcohol abuse (Lawlis 69).

It was by chance that I found marijuana in my son's room. I was shocked, disappointed, and upset with myself because I didn't know. I missed the signs and felt like I had let him down by not being there. His grades were all good and his teachers all praised his work, but I should have recognized the signs. I surprisingly remained calm when I questioned him about what I had

found. He informed me that he had started using marijuana when he was living with his other mother, around his freshman year of high school. He told me that I could ask him any questions I saw fit. I ought not have been surprised because he seemed to be struggling with depression for quite a while and I had wanted him to attend counseling but he refused. He had turned to drugs to feel better or feel nothing at all. I made sure that he knew that I didn't like the behavior, but that I loved him. Sometimes that is all you can do. There are no perfect parents. I am happy to report that he no longer smokes marijuana, and I'm so proud of him. As parents you can never give up on your kids.

I grew up in a town where virtually everyone drank alcohol. I began drinking alcohol during my sixth-grade year. I look at six-graders now and they look like babies. My parents drank every night at home, as did most of the parents of my friends. I now wonder if all these parents met the requirements for functioning alcoholics. When I went to college, I drank a lot. I was back home one weekend and got stopped for careless driving and taken to the local police station. My dad came and got me, not saying a whole lot. I do remember my mom telling me the police had told my dad that if they didn't get me under control, they were going to lose me. I slowed down my drinking a lot,and I realized that once I took that one too many drinks there was no going back. The problem was, I didn't realize when that one drink too many happened. Now, if I drink on a rare occasion, I allow myself two drinks and no more. Luckily, I didn't repeat the habits of my parents who drank nightly. My sons have maybe seen me drink less than a handful of times in their lives, so hopefully I've set a good example for them, and they will make good decisions if they choose to drink alcohol.

Our kids are always watching us whether we realize it or not. Teenagers need guidance on how to manage stress and how to deal with difficult situations. According to Dr. Frank Lawlis (69), If you don't provide positive role models through you or someone else, teens will find and copy negative role models, including those who might use drugs, abuse alcohol, or indulge in other self-destructive behaviors.

Today's teenagers need every available resource because of the intense pressures they face. Help your child develop emotional intelligence so they can determine who is trustworthy and who is not, and so they know what they must do to win the trust of others. Teach your child to reach out to others in need and to put into relationships as much as, or more than, they take out (Lawlis 164). Help them develop these emotional intelligence skills(EI) or (EQ). Some people feel that EI /EQ intelligence is equally as important as IQ or even more so. Emotional Intelligence is the ability to manage both your own emotions and understand the emotions of people around you. High EI /EQ overlaps with strong interpersonal skills , especially in the areas of conflict management and communication. Emotional intelligence most often includes four attributes: self-management, self-awareness, social awareness ,and relationship management. EI/EQ can be improved with thoughtful practice. First,the next time your child feels angry ask them these questions: Why are you angry? Did someone upset you? Was it their intent to hurt you? Allowing yourself time to think about these questions without lashing out first, often avoids conflict altogether. Next,think about your strengths and weaknesses. No one is good at everything. There is no shame in asking for help if you need it. I 've always told my students that there will always be someone better at things than you and there will always be someone worse at certain things than you,but the important thing is to be the best you can be. There is no need for anyone to compare themselves to others. Third, put an effort into understanding what people are communicating nonverbally through their tone or facial gestures. Lastly, work on communicating effectively. Get to your main point quickly. Cut parts from your message that aren't necessarily relevant to the person you are talking to. Also, give full attention to someone when they are speaking, including eye contact. People with high EI/EQ often have strong interpersonal skills especially in the areas of conflict management and communication which are both crucial skills in the workplace.

Parents must be more involved, not only in your child's life but in their education, kindergarten through graduation. When students are in elementary school, parents are often at school and active in the school's PTA or PTO organizations. However, as students get older the lack of parent involvement seems to dwindle. When I was an elementary school principal, I would meet once a month with the PTO, listen to their ideas, answer questions, and address concerns. Even then with a student body of around 500, it was the same ten parents each month. More parents need to be involved to support teachers and open lines of communication. Reach out to the school and offer any help that you feel comfortable giving. Realize that teachers are there to help students, and any parental help or support you can give them the better it is for the student. Be a partner with the school and your child's teachers. Be careful if talking negatively about the school or your child's teacher because our kids are always listening, and they learn by copying adults. Please try to change your mindset about teachers being babysitters or only being in education because they don't work during June, July and August. It is more noticeable in small communities, but most teachers must get another job in the summer to make ends meet.

Please have your child school-ready with basic life skills when they first enter education. As I spoke with a kindergarten teacher just recently she shared that several students come to school without being potty trained and had no medical reason for this. This speaks volumes about parent involvement or lack of it. It is unreasonable for parents to believe it is a school's responsibility to teach their children these skills. Parents should be embarrassed to send their students to school like this. I believe that this is setting their child up for being bullied and is borderline parental neglect. This specific teacher retired earlier than she had intended due to this issue.

Another area that seems to borderline on neglect is when parents send their kids to school dirty. There are so many places where showers can be taken and clothes washed. Many schools have washers and dryers in the building, often located in the nurse or social workers office. All schools have showers available; it is the parents responsibility to ask. When a child or their clothes are dirty at school, it affects every part of them: physically, emotionally, and mentally. If a student doesn't feel good about who they are they will not be focused on academics. If a student doesn't have any friends,they will not be able to put their best effort into learning. Parents, don't set your kids up for failure. I recently worked with a senior who was a great kid, but she had a terrible home environment. Several people lived in a house that did not always have running water or electricity, and food was sometimes scarce.

She worked hard at academics and had a job outside of school. She lost one of her jobs due to a uniform violation. I had to have a difficult conversation with her, explaining that uniform and dress includes proper hygiene; she often smelled. She would sometimes walk to the community center to shower, but when the temperatures got cold that wasn't always an option. When things became hostile between her and her father she left home. Because she was 18 there was nothing her father could do. She moved in with her boyfriend and his family in another town. She visited today and looked so good and happy. She was clean, had new clothes, and her hair was neat and combed. She told me that she had been showering everyday. I was so glad and thought to myself that she didn't even realize that this is what usually happens within families. I am elated for her. She graduates next week due partly to the teachers working with her and understanding her situation. I explained to her this was because she was such a good, and respectful person; otherwise the teachers may not have cared.

Walter Edward Williams , professor at George Mason University, said, "For somebody to do well in school, somebody needs to make him go to bed on time and get a good 10 hours of sleep. Someone must make him do his homework. Somebody must feed him breakfast in the morning, and somebody must make him mind the teacher. If these things are not done, I don't care how much money you put into the school system, education will not occur." Parents, will you be that somebody?

Parenting shouldn't stop in the summer. Statistics tell us that the summer slide occurs. Summer slide is where students don't do anything academically during the summer, and they lose school skills. "In general, kids learn a lot more in kindergarten, first and second grade than kids in middle school or high school, because learning follows a curve where it's accelerated early in life and then plateaus," says James Kim, Ed. D., an assistant professor of education at Harvard University. "Things like decoding, letter knowledge, and word reading skills are very susceptible to decay without frequent practice, as are math facts like addition and subtraction," (Austrew 2022). Parents can help by keeping their kids engaged in reading and math during the summer to avoid the summer slide. Parents must have students read if only for twenty minutes a day. Allow the students to read the books they want to read, not the ones you choose. Students will be more likely to read if the topic interests them. Parents should also include time for smart play. According to Scholastic, " things such as games and puzzles are a great way to brush up on the basics." Get out of the house and take your kids to museums, historical sites, or even parks. Help teach your child money skills, like counting change or identifying coins. Use dice for addition and subtraction, cook together, or teach fractions with measuring cups. Be creative and make learning fun. This increases learning and lessens the summer slide impact, but also creates memories for you and your child. Let your students use their imagination by building forts out of boxes or blankets, playing with Legos, and building simple projects out of popsicle sticks. Visit the local library together; books are free for all who visit, and during and library staff lead summer months programs and crafts. Year round, students can get free books through Dolly Parton's Imagination Library. This is available in most states for students under school age. All a parent must do is sign up, which takes about two minutes. You can do this at your local library or online.

According to Kate Barrington, from Public School Review 2003, teachers in public schools can only do so much to support their students. When students go home for the day, the state of their home life impacts their personal and academic development. Students who I currently work with can function relatively well during the school day with support in place; however, when they go home, many gains made during the school day become erased, and the trust and learning process start all over the next day. It seems like one step forward and two steps back. As parents we must try to provide a stable and nurturing environment. If you cannot do this as a parent, reach out to available resources such as your child's school. If they can not help ,they will provide resources, names, and places that may.. This website may be a great place to start: https://dese.mo.gov/college-career-readiness/school-counseling/traumainformed.

In some cases, parents may lack the ability to offer their children academic assistance; however, entities such as schools, churches, local universities,after-school programs, Khan Academy, and online resources provide tutoring. Parents must be engaged enough to facilitate this if their student is struggling.

Mental health issues prevail now more than ever. Many believe the world-wide quarantine during COVID-19 contributed to the mental health crisis. Because of the resulting solitude, parents must prioritize talking to their children and keeping open the lines of communication. If parents believe that their child is experiencing mental health issues, seek help for them through the school or outside agencies. Don't forget to communicate with the school about these issues as well. I do believe progress has been to lessen the negative stigma associated with mental health issues; but more needs to be done to make these issues more visible and more acceptable. This should be no different than going to the doctor for a stomach ache. Our government, doctors, sports figures, and other role models must continue to make facing mental health issues less taboo and more acceptable. Stress scales and tips on how to reduce stress are provided at the back of this book.

Parents and the school system need to be partners, and parents must stop enabling their children. There is a fine line between being present and available and not being an enabler. I heard a story recently about a young man in rehabilitation. He got kicked out because his mother and sister snuck a vape into him while he was in rehab. Was this parent actually thinking she was helping her son? I'm not sure some parents should be parents.

Just because you biologically can have children doesn't mean you should. Parenting is a 24/7 job that lasts at least 18 years and demands serious consideration. Case in point: Because my partner and I were a gay couple and used a fertility doctor to conceive our boys, we were required to visit a psychologist before the doctor would perform the insemination. We had to be cleared as acceptable potential parents and obtain a stamp of approval before we could proceed. I believe anyone wanting to become parents should have to go through a similar vetting practice. I realize that this would be nearly impossible to enact. My point is, some people should deeply examine themselves before having kids.

As a parent, you must practice tough love and accept that your child may be mad at you. Parents must monitor their children's social media accounts. Social media has made bullying easier by allowing bullies to hide behind their words, and it gives them constant access to their prey. I know teenagers view this as an invasion of their privacy. You are just doing your parental job, trying to protect them.

Society as a whole must do a better job identifying bullies, recognizing those who have been bullied, and harshly punishing those doing the bullying. Bullies exist in all facets of life, including the workplace. Many of the school shooting suspects were victims of bullying themselves and didn't believe they received the justice they deserved.

I currently teach a student who dropped out of school because he was bullied and is currently going to school online. He is a junior, and his parents were concerned about his socialization skills and his ability to secure and maintain employment after graduation. He recently started coming to school for my career lab class. He gets so anxious when he sees a crowd of students and recognizes some of them as the ones who bullied him. He waits in the attendance office, and I go down and escort him to the classroom before we head off to his job. He has made great strides at work, works well with one or two other people at a time, and listens to most adults without hesitation. Because of these successes, he has started to attend a geometry class within the school. Bottom line, we all need to remember being bullied can be debilitating!

Here is an example of bullying gone horribly wrong: A New Jersey teenager was bullied and assaulted at her high school and the entire incident was posted online. Two days after the online posting, she committed suicide. Her parents sued the school, alleging school district officials were aware of the bullying and violence culture at the high school yet failed to protect their daughter. Four students were criminally charged for this incident, and the district superintendent resigned. Her parents said that the assault and video publicly humiliated their daughter leading to her suicide (Helsel 2024).

We certainly don't need parents taking matters into their own hands, like Jennifer Rossi, a mother from Texas. She was angry that another student took her son's drink. The next day she made a mixture of lemon juice, vinegar, salt, and Gatorade for her son to deliver to the bully. Although no permanent harm was done to the bully, he was hospitalized and Rossi was arrested (Haworth 2024).

Other than bullying there are so many reasons why a parent should monitor their children's social media accounts. Sexual predators use social media to target teenagers ,identity theft occurs online, and sex trafficking can begin innocently enough while students are on social media.

Parents also need to be mindful of their children's physical health because we are creating a nation of unhealthy children. Poor eating habits and lack of physical activity due to students' engagement with electronics are creating a nation of overweight youth. Most schools require at least one unit of physical education to graduate high school. Some parents and students think that this is unreasonable. I recommend we increase that to four units of physical education to meet graduation requirements. I realize that some students have limitations and physical activity is painful to them and of course, there are exceptions to all rules. Many schools have added walking, dance, weightlifting, or aerobic classes to help with options for those students who might struggle. A school in Dubuque, Iowa allows students to receive physical education credits by doing yard work for senior citizens and people with disabilities (Mac 2022). Perhaps adding a cycling class might be another option: we simply think outside of the box.

On the website below is good information including a resource guide for parents and caregivers. Here is the National Suicide Prevention Lifeline 800-273-8255. This resource includes a document to help your child.

https://dese.mo.gov/college-career-readiness/school-counseling/trama

Summary

Parents have always had a tough job raising their kids, but today's students are under more stress than ever. Teenagers experiment with drugs, alcohol, and sex. As their brains rewire themselves, they lack empathy and understanding of their actions and how they relate to future ramifications. COVID-19 had an impact on all of us but seems to have harmed students' mental health. As a parent, you must monitor this and get your student help through the school or a private agency. Parents must remain present in their students' lives even though they may try to push you away. Make sure you are there for support but do not become an enabler.

Parents need to monitor their student's social media accounts. Parents need to monitor their children's activity levels as well. Sedentary students staying on electronics constantly is causing a nation of overweight youth.

Parents must stay involved and partner with the school. Schools can't do everything by themselves and often are too proud to ask for help. You can do a lot to help your students do homework and review school concepts during the summer, especially in reading and math. The local library is a great source of information.

Bullying continues to be a problem and social media has just heightened the ability to bully twenty-four hours a day. Students need to make sure that they let adults know about bullying. Schools need to have a zero-tolerance policy for bullying. Every child deserves to feel safe at school and every parent should not have to worry about their child being bullied.

Parents must be positive role models because students are looking for role models and if you don't provide this, they will find a role model who may not portray positive attributes. Be present.

Considerations for Teachers

Teacher retention is a serious problem. By some estimates, approximately 40% of teachers leave the teaching profession within five years of starting to teach while 50% leave within six years. Districts must bear the cost to hire thousands of well-qualified people every year, only to have them leave. This is a lose-lose situation, counterproductive, bad for the school, bad for the teachers , but most importantly bad for the students. Yet research shows that the single most important factor in improving student achievement is great teaching (Chilcott 2010 as cited Weber 2010). I don't believe that I even felt like I was an effective teacher until after my fifth year of teaching. Those that leave the field so early haven't really given it a chance.

Almost everyone seems to have a story about how one teacher got through to them, changed, and reshaped their life forever. Teachers, more than facilities or a great gym or classroom size, that stand out in every great school. "Could it be that teaching is just about the most important job in the world" (Chilcott 2010 as cited by Weber 2010)? As Joe Sanfelippo, superintendent for Fall Creek Schools in Wisconsin says, "It is more about the connection than the content. Every interaction matters because every interaction could be the one they talk about forever." For me, my first-grade teacher Mrs. Brown was amazing. She had that unique ability to make each and every student feel special and important. Her husband, although not a teacher, possessed the same special qualities. He dressed up like Santa at Christmas and surprised us at school and did many other special things for us. When I was in the fifth grade, I remember the teachers telling us that while they were on vacation, Mr. and Mrs. Brown stopped to help a stranded driver. That driver shot them both, killing Mr. Brown. Mrs. Brown survived but suffered a brain injury and a long recovery. I still remember her even 50 years later. Author Maya Angelou said, "People will forget what you said. People will forget what you did. But people will never forget how you made them feel." Fortunately, I had several teachers after Mrs. Brown who were great at their jobs, which is probably why I love education and being an educator.

It doesn't have to be a teacher who students make a connection with. It can be any adult in your building. Vice principal Arnold Ford of Master Charter School in Philadelphia, Pennsylvania, loves his job in education as well and doesn't think twice about hugging his students to show he cares. I have a few students at middle school and high school who want hugs. One student affectionately refers to me as his grandma. I recently missed school for a few days due to illness; when I returned, he ran up to me in the hall, said that he had missed me, gave me a big hug, and then told me he loved me. I told him I loved him too. Appropriate physical touch is important and acceptable at all levels. Of course, do it in a public place. Statistics tell us that people can survive without sex but cannot survive without touch. If a student wants to or needs to hug you, hug them; it is not appropriate for the adult to initiate the hug. Connect to the emotion. They don't care how much you know until they know how much you care.

Joe Sanfilippo says, "We must bring that small school feeling to every school. Secondary schools should be small enough or divided into small enough units to allow teachers and staff to get to know all students as individuals and respond to their specific learning needs." There should be someone in each building who makes students feel safe and they can connect with. Be yourself with students. If students see you as a real person, it is so much easier to make a connection with them. Laugh at yourself and laugh with the students. Many teachers try to put on a staunch demeanor. It used to be said that you shouldn't smile until Christmas, but this doesn't apply anymore. More students than ever do not have positive adult role models in their lives, so we must make positive connections with our students as soon as possible.

Some teachers are wonderful at content knowledge and delivering that knowledge to students so they understand. However, they might fall short on the **making connections** part of teaching. My son in high school had a high stakes computer technologies test for college credit, an Algebra II test, and a history EOC (end of course assessment) test all on the same day. He did great on his computer certification test; we don't know the EOC results yet, but he got a D on his algebra test. He has carried a high B, low A on all assignments and tests this year in Algebra II. We were both upset about his score. ! asked him to say something to his teacher about retakes or test corrections,which he did. The answer was no, there was nothing else he could do. I understand that if this is a rule, the teacher must stand behind it. But if you know your students and know this is uncharacteristic of them, why would you not want to know what happened on the test, especially if the student asks?

Many secondary schools have added a 30-to 40 minute period throughout the day, so teachers and students can get to know each other. This period is also to assist students with assignments. Secondary students are sometimes reluctant to talk, so many teachers just give up and use this time as an extra plan period for them and a study hall for the students, thus missing the opportunity to make that important connection. As teachers, we must get students talking. I brought in Scruple cards and read appropriate scenarios and we would discuss them. There were no right or wrong answers. Some of these questions asked "what would you do if" or whether they thought something was fair. Examples of this could be if you heard a neighbor in your apartment building yelling for help as if they were being beaten up, what would you do? If a student was forced to cut their hair in a particular way to play a sport, is this fair? Jenny Woo invented a deck of cards called, "52 Essential Conversations," where each card has two questions, an icebreaker, and a longer prompt designed to prompt deeper conversations. One example of a card's icebreaker question asks you to describe who you are and how others see you. The longer prompt is designed to promote social awareness and asks you to think of two other people you know and consider how you're alike and different from them (Sauer 2024). These cards are all right in line with emotional intelligence that we previously talked about. Oftentimes, I just listen to what the students are talking about and jump into their conversation. They may think I'm a nosy or a crazy old lady, but I don't care because I'm making connections. The students know they matter to me. I also believe that we are missing the opportunity by not utilizing cooks, custodians, counselors, paraprofessionals, secretaries, and all other school personnel when facilitating these groups. The more these individuals become involved and the creation of smaller groups, increases the chance for that all-important connection. The fact that bullying continues to be a big problem is another reason why each student should have at least one trusted adult in every building. Keep in mind that you, the teacher, may be doing nothing wrong if students are not willing to discuss. Some groups are just easier to have discussions with. Do not give up just because it is not easy.

At middle school and some high schools periodically, there are lessons or topics to discuss in your thirty to forty-minute get-to-know-you period. The other day at middle school the topic was bullying. A teacher said to me that they didn't know how to teach this because she was a non-core teacher. Usually, with a prescribed lesson all the materials are prepared for you; you just facilitate the discussion. Importantly, you are a **teacher** of **students;** art, music, and physical education are merely subjects. Perhaps for a teacher like this, topic cards mentioned above. would be helpful.

Some schools have grade levels divided into teams of core subject teachers (math,science,social studies, language arts, and reading) who all share the same students. This allows these teachers to get to know the students and exchange information about students with each other. Teachers discuss the students and missing assignments, strengths and weaknesses, and changes in behavior.

Lack of involvement in communication by the students at both the middle school and high school made me realize that maybe not all teachers know how to question students and initiate conversations. *J.T. Dillon's Questioning and Teaching: A Manual of Practice* (1988) still seems as relevant today as ever in observations and the differences between questioning for recitation and questioning for discussion. "Questioning for recitation is no less important in teaching and learning than questioning for discussion. Questioning in recitation checks for understanding. Such questions determine if students are ready to move forward or if they need reteaching. Not only does questioning in recitation provide teachers with feedback, but, when properly managed, it also engages students in reflecting on the extent to which they know or understand facts and concepts. Self-assessment is the most powerful type of formative assessment. Where questioning in recitation checks for understanding, questioning for discussion helps to build a deeper understanding" (Dillion 1998 as cited by Walsh and Sattes 2015).

There are certainly some topics that will ignite students into discussion (McCann 2014 as cited by Sattes and Walsh 2015), "points to topics adolescents will energetically tackle and begin discussing quite passionately -equality, justice, responsibility, freedom, and compassion". I believe it is important to include social media, and to be more specific, cell phones, TikTok, and Snapchat, especially as it relates to being allowed in school.

The most important expectation to communicate is the belief that each student should be prepared to contribute. Carefully crafted participation norms build a culture in which students accept responsibility for their own and others' engagement in the classroom. In the beginning, teachers might have to draw fair sticks or call on individuals. Teachers must lead students in developing and honoring norms that create equity. Through these discussion skills and established norms, we can begin to realize and be accepting or tolerant of others ideas and beliefs. Structures that scaffold participation by all can help normalize expected behaviors and assist students to become increasingly responsible for their own and their classmates' participation. Another technique teachers utilize to get participation from everyone is brainwriting. Brainwriting is similar to brainstorming with the difference being everyone writes their ideas down rather than sharing their ideas verbally. The teacher then reads these anonymous suggestions to the class for discussion and consensus.

Most students don't come to school with the skills required for questioning and discussion. Teachers must model the use of questioning that leads to a productive discussion. (Dillion 1988 as cited as Walsh and Sattes 2015), "concluded that teacher intervention during student discussions tends to shut down student thinking and student talk. He found this to be particularly true of positive feedback or praise. This is because when a teacher communicates agreement with one student's thinking, both the speaker and other students in the class determine that there is no need for further thought. After all, the teacher has gotten the answer they were after".

"Students must believe that their teacher does not have a preconceived best answer or preferred position. Teachers must be careful not to impose their views or perspectives on their students" (Dillion 1988 as cited by Walsh and Sattes 2015). We live in a culture in which silence has become uncomfortable and awkward, so students need to become comfortable with silence. Students must understand the purpose of the pause or silence, to think.

I included questioning and communication skills because everyone in today's world seems so angry. We must learn how to listen politely to other people's perspectives, and if we disagree with them, be okay with that without getting upset. Becoming upset just because you disagree with someone can lead to bullying and school shootings. Stephen R. Covey says, "The biggest communication problem is we do not listen to understand, we listen to reply." This is the main reason I also believe that every high school student should be required to take debate class. According to an online dictionary the definition of debate is" a formal discussion on a particular topic in a public meeting or legislative assembly, in which opposing arguments are put forward." It is so important that we can see more than one side to every situation; debate teaches us how to express ourselves, listen to others' ideas, and be cordial to each other even if we strongly disagree. Kindness, respect, and tolerance need to be part of the curriculum as much as all other academics. Students learn respect when they see respect. As a society we must devise a way for everyone to co-exist and be civil to each other. Teachers can only do so much at school. Consider our 2020 presidential debates when opponents ridiculed and belittled each other. Is this the kind of behavior we want our students to emulate? Whether we mean for them to or not, young adults learn by watching/hearing adults. Look at the January 6, 2021, insurrection as well as the way members of Congress act toward each other; young adults see this on the news or read about it and believe it to be acceptable. Everyone wants to hurt others they disagree with. Why is this tolerated? How is this okay that elected officials, our noblesse oblige,who act more like thugs than the distinguished representatives that they are supposed to be, are allowed to keep their jobs? Why do we allow this to happen? If you or I were to act like this at our job, we would be strongly reprimanded or fired! It seems the information about emotional intelligence discussed in the Considerations for Parents section of this book may need to be studied by our political leaders. As adults, we must condemn these actions if we care about our youth and the future of our country. We must take a stand and be vocal that we no longer will accept this behavior. Talk to everyone you can.Only through actions by great numbers of people will cause change to occur. Some believe we are close to another civil war. We can no longer sit back and watch our democracy self-destruct. Make your voice heard,talk to legislators, and demand they do better. We can not let our students, our future, continue to imitate this behavior.

I love to watch NFL football, specifically the KC Chiefs. These professional athletes beat up each other on the field. They want to win and will do just about anything to make that happen, but after the game they talk, shake hands, and trade jerseys. If these men who are trained and paid to be physical can turn it off when the game is over, why can't everyone else? Peaceful protests are what our country was built on, not violence. Look how much Martin Luther King Jr., and his followers were able to facilitate change through peaceful methods. We must return to this. Adults must act like respectable citizens, not only to model for our children, but to make the world better and safer again. "No matter what happens in life, be good to people, being good to people is a wonderful legacy to leave behind," a poignant quote by Taylor Swift. Teachers cannot be the only ones teaching kindness and respect.

If we are going to work on communication skills with our students, we need to make sure we are communicating with our parents/guardians. I have heard teachers say they were not calling a certain parent because the parent will probably be rude to them. If you are doing what is best for the student, you must put your fears and biases aside and contact the parent. You are a professional. If the parent becomes rude or curses at you, say good-bye and hang up knowing you did the right thing by making the call for the betterment of the student. We should not be afraid of parents.

The information that follows is from Emily Erisman, M. LPC., during our conversation in May 2024. “When I began my career in 2001, the overall climate of education was remarkably different. Some of the differences vary or are hardly noticeable, such as : levels of parent engagement , quality of teacher training, and professional dress standards. Other differences present constant obstacles to teaching directly and affect the quality of education for our students. The biggest difference I notice is the **mindset** of a greater majority of the students and the parents who come into our building. The parents and students believe that they are in charge. Over the years, in schools' efforts to accommodate everyone's preferences, we've inadvertently evolved into being a customer service profession. In doing so, we've sacrificed the quality of education."

During my first couple years of teaching, I was assigned to the bus lane for after-school duty. We had a no-gum-chewing policy in the building and on the bus. We were finding chewed gum all around the building and stuck to bus seats. As a student exited the building chewing gum, I asked them to spit the gum into the trash can or they would be written up. When that student got home, I don't know what the student told their mother, but that mom called the school and wanted to talk to me. When I answered the phone, I tried to explain to the mother what had occurred. The mother started cursing at me, not allowing me to talk. I eventually hung up on her. The next morning my principal called me in and asked if I had hung up on a parent. I sheepishly answered that I had. He said, "You probably should have hung up earlier. Never allow a parent to talk to you like that." I was certainly relieved. I believed I was going to be in trouble. I understand that chewing gum isn't the end of the world, but it was a rule, put in place for a purpose, and it needed to be followed.

If we are to make real connections with each student, the student and their teacher need to determine their learning styles. Are they visual, auditory, or kinesthetic learners? For the students, knowing this information will help them be able to process and recall information better. For teachers, knowing this information will help them design their lessons differently appropriately to tailor the individual assignments toward the students' strengths based on their learning styles. Many learning styles inventories are available for all ages and most of them are free.

I believe that we water down our curriculum and don't challenge most students enough. There is a lot of wasted time in the school day. (Beers and Probst 2012). Part of the problem exists in the misinterpretation of the term " rigor". Rigor is not an attribute of a text but rather a characteristic of our behavior with that text. A professional football player lifting a 100-pound weight ten times would not be justified in calling that a rigorous workout; an eighth grader trying to get into shape for the football team probably would. The fourth grader, who could not lift the weight at all, would, like the professional football player, be hard-pressed to have said his workout was rigorous. The quality, and rigor, aren't in the barbell but in the interaction with it. Rigor, in other words, lies in the transaction between the reader and the text and then among readers. The essence of rigor is engagement and commitment" (Beers and Probst 2012). A classroom that respects what the students bring to it, what they are capable of and interested in, and that welcomes them into an active intellectual community is more likely to achieve that rigor.

A challenge for educators, who have deep experience in their disciplinary content, must remember what it feels like to be a very new learner without a background in the subject. We as teachers see connections and meaning in the content, and this can be challenging for a new learner (Posey 59).

It is important to realize that emotions play a large part in learning.Socrates said, "Education is the kindling of a flame, not the filling of a vessel." Brain-based teaching strategies focus on the social-emotional needs of learners (Posey 4).

Students who have not experienced success in your field, or any field, will be hesitant and nervous until they understand or a connection with the content, the teacher, or they experience success. Educators have a choice about how to make the material relevant, relatable, and engaging while building background knowledge so students can show what they know.

Engagement involves increased focus, participation, and interest. Students give more effort and persist through challenges when they are engaged (Posey 7). Teachers must remember that every learning event in our classroom is based on the unique experiences and backgrounds that each student brings. In our nation, classroom populations today are more diverse than ever before.

Posey further states that "a one-size-fits-all lesson is unlikely to address the range of experiences that our students with diverse backgrounds bring. For example, if the goal is to deliver an effective oral report and meaningful connections are made to how these skills are relevant, then consider how you can offer a few options for students to select as they work to achieve the goal. Maybe there is an option to deliver the presentation to the class or to make a video of their presentation, like a news report. You might offer the option to use a graphic organizer and to preview the rubric/scoring guide that will be used to assess the oral delivery." These options should be available for all learners. Such availability allows all learners to build a repertoire of strategies to become experts in their strengths, challenges, and weaknesses.

I realize this requires a little more preparation on the teachers' part, but if you truly want the students to be able to show what they know and give an equal playing field to all, this should be happening in every classroom. Many teachers will allow students with IEPs to complete fewer questions, but the rest of the assignment is the same as all the students. That is not always what is best for the students. IEP stands for individualized education plan, not just a shortened version of the same assignment, unless the IEP specifically states this. Far too many teachers are quickly handed a copy of the paperwork for these identified students and are expected to read it, understand it, and implement it. It is a lot added to an already full plate. The special education teacher (case manager) who oversees each student's paperwork, should spend time with the regular education teacher to explain more clearly the accommodations and modifications and to help alleviate some of the additional stress associated with having an IEP student. A co-teacher in the classroom will make it much easier when you have an IEP student in your classroom. Unfortunately, every class with IEP students will not have a co-teacher. Paraprofessionals are very helpful as well, if the district can employ enough paras to provide support. Like the teacher shortage, there is a paraprofessional shortage as well. Teachers don't intentionally overlook making accommodations or allowing modifications; but because they have so many other things to concentrate on, like state standards,they become overwhelmed or perhaps were never properly trained. As always, just as we tell our students, if you don't understand how to implement some of these modifications, just ask questions.

Special education teachers are more than willing to help in any way they can. However, they too are overwhelmed with the constantly changing rules that govern IEP's along with the mandated paperwork that seems endless and timelines that seem impossible to meet.

Regular education and special education teachers must work together to achieve the greatest gains from **their** students. I believe some regular education teachers still see IEP students as only the special education teacher's responsibility .

I believe we should just let teachers teach. Teachers are the experts in their field. I also believe sometimes teachers miss out on teachable moments because they don't think they can veer from the information that they must deliver. I might argue that some of the teachable moments help build background knowledge and make understanding the content being taught easier for students to comprehend. Just like in my self-contained room, I had to teach several different levels to different students based on their abilities. All teachers should be doing this in the classroom.

"Everybody is a genius. But if you judge a fish by its ability to climb a tree, it will live its whole life believing that it is stupid", stated Albert Einstein. Too often we expect our students' brains to be mostly the same, but they are not. Brains are as unique as our fingerprints (Posey 36).

We all vary in how we best demonstrate knowledge and understanding in different contexts. When we require students to show what they know in just one way, we often create unintended barriers for them to show their understanding. One educator noted, “If you are not being intentionally inclusive, you are being exclusive” (Posey 37). Every student should be taught like they have an IEP because each student is unique.

Learning is dependent on the interaction between the individual and the environment, and because each person’s brain network is unique, we must design intentionally and flexibly for the range of learners. The more proactively we can do this, the less reteaching we will need to do, and the more inclusive our learning environments will be from the outset. Therefore, it is essential to design options so new learners can build relevant backgrounds, be strategic and goal-oriented, and be engaged and empowered to take on more complex learning.

Most teachers are hardworking and try to do the best they can in the classroom. But like all human beings, teachers respond to incentives that are placed in front of them; unfortunately current public education systems focus more on data than high student achievement for all.. So, when educational decisions are being made, they may or may not be guided by the goal of maximizing student learning (Hanushek 2009 as cited by Weber 2010). Finding great teachers is the "secret sauce" of great schools (Canada 1998 as cited by Weber 2010).

According to Geoffrey Canada in his book, *Bringing Change to Scale: The Next Big Reform Challenge*, "If a school is staffed with great teachers, it must have the ability to retain and reward excellence." Teachers who understand their value is acknowledged through compensation, both monetary and symbolic, recognize they are part of a system whose leadership is focused on the end goal of student success. In contrast, where teachers work hard to deliver results but are not appreciated nor rewarded, they become disheartened and will inevitably leave the school or drop out of the profession altogether. Even the small tokens of recognition and rewards make teachers feel appreciated.

Teachers in Newton, Massachusetts, have been on strike, but not only for higher wages. According to an article written by Hanna Panreck for Fox News on February 1, 2024, the Newton Teachers Association has spent every minute of the strike trying to reopen the school. The goal all along was to return students to the classroom, but teachers can no longer accept the working conditions that put students at risk and don't meet their needs. The NTA stresses that without aides and behavior therapists, many students cannot reach their full potential. Similarly, without easy access to a social worker, a student's mental health crisis can escalate. However, with the current wages offered by Newton, qualified individuals cannot afford to take those jobs. Other districts are in a similar situation to the Newton School District and wonder what it will take to invoke change.

In June 2024, both Louisiana and Oklahoma announced the Ten Commandments must be posted in all classrooms within their states. Oklahoma extended their mandate to include grades

5-12 to have a Bible within each classroom and the educator to teach from it as part of the curriculum. Ryan Walters, the superintendent of Oklahoma schools stated the Bible as " one of the most historically significant books and a cornerstone of Western civilization"(Evans 2024). There are so many things wrong with these mandates inside public schools: separation of church and state, but most importantly added responsibilities to the plates of teachers who are barely hanging on.

We need to rethink how we pay teachers so we can attract and maintain the best. Teachers make an average of $3600 less than ten years ago, adjusted for inflation (www.nea.org). Teachers should receive **starting** salaries in the $50,000- $60,000 range at a minimum. Nationally, 2022-2023, the average teacher salary is $66,745. The average teacher salary in Missouri is $51,557. Nationally, teachers earn 25% more on average in collective bargaining states (NEA Rankings & Estimates 2023). Teachers should be paid like full-time employees but should be required to work full-time hours. Most teachers work well past when the students have left for the day anyway. The United States has a shorter school year as compared to other countries. The average number of school days in the United States is 180 and in Japan, it is 243 days. If teacher salaries were raised to appropriate levels, there most likely would not be a teacher shortage. Those who ignored their passion for pay would become the teachers they should have been all along.

I believe that we should have year-round school. This would allow students to receive nutritional meals year-round. Scheduled breaks throughout the year would equal current summer break and subsequent days off during the year. The knowledge students would maintain will eliminate some remedial and reteaching work. Summer break is typically a time for kids to have zero responsibility that only comes with being young. Ashley Austrew, for Scholastic, August 2022, reports that all this free time can lead to summer slide, a regression in academic proficiency, and experts warn it is hindering kids' progress when they head back to school in the fall. The study showed that kids lose significant knowledge in reading and math over summer break, which snowballs each year. A more recent study of children in the third to fifth grades also showed that students lost on average about twenty percent of their school-year gains in reading and twenty- seven percent in math. Younger kids, second grade or under, experience the most learning loss.

Adding time to the school day would be beneficial. The added days to the school year or the extra time after school could be devoted to reteaching concepts to those who have not mastered them or teaching accelerated curriculum to those who have mastered the key concepts. Another option would be teaching a topic of interest to the student, something not even part of the curriculum that the student and teacher could bond over and enjoy together.

Teachers overwhelmingly believe that top-quality professional development is crucial to their continuing education/development. Great teachers are always excited about learning new ways they can help their students learn. Teachers also want more feedback about their performance in the classroom (Gates 2009 as cited by Weber 2010). Teachers deserve quality feedback about their teaching and need to be validated. Administrators must make time to be in teachers' classrooms more than once a year and for more than five minutes. This should be an expectation. At the beginning of the school year, as a principal, I would schedule on my calendar the dates and times I was going to be in each teacher's classroom to do an observation. I would not deviate from this schedule unless there was an emergency.

When I moved to the elementary school as principal, I had some very nervous teachers because I was in their classrooms often. The previous principal had not done this. I quickly explained that I just wanted to be knowledgeable of the happenings in their classroom. At faculty meetings, I was able to share specific examples of great teaching I saw in a certain teacher's room. The teachers soon learned I was paying attention and giving them praise. If I saw something that was a concern, we talked about it in private.

> Schools begin with teachers. That sounds easy enough, but great teachers are not as plentiful as you might expect. "Put enough great teachers together under the leadership of a teacher who understands all the ingredients of learning and something very good will happen" (Matthews 2009 as cited by Weber 2010). A super school must be exciting and involving, where students want to come to school and do the hard work it takes to learn. This requires teachers who know how to inject joy and suspense into lessons. Barrington Irving, a pilot, and educator speaks to this when talking about his nonprofit, Experience Aviation. "Meaningful real-world experiences fire up the neurons in

kids' minds. Many students end up bored and disengaged from the curriculum and we lose them (National Geographic)" and if teachers aren't mindful this will result in boreout. "Boreout is the emotional deadening one feels when under-stimulated"(Grant 130).Unfortunately,in today's world, students must be entertained to be engaged, a side effect of playing video games. We want schools where students rebel if teachers just give them worksheet after worksheet. We want students to hold the teachers to engaging lessons.John Holdren-President Obama's science advisor, is quoted as saying,"We wouldn't teach football from a textbook. It is even more important that America's youth should learn math and science by doing"(Schwarz 2005 as cited by Weber 2010).For thousands of years, people have learned by doing, through hands-on experience.Jean Piaget researched and wrote about the "concrete operational stage" of learning where children begin to make abstract connections based on concrete experiences.

I believe most teachers are trying to adjust their teaching styles to keep students more engaged. I was recently interviewed by a student at the middle school I currently work in. The student was a "doctor" from her science class, and she was asking me about my symptoms and taking notes as she questioned me. Before the student interview, I had been given a script by the teacher with my symptoms.The student was then to research to determine what ailment I had. I thought this was a great lesson. Another teacher recently reviewed an upcoming quiz by putting the students into groups, allowing the students to pick team names, and playing "Deal or no Deal."The students had fun playing while gaining mastery of the subject matter. I'm a firm believer the more learning mimics a game the greater chance of student participation and learning."Play is not a frivolous activity-it's a source of joy and a path to mastery" (Grant 150).

I am in a unique position teaching both middle school and high school and have the opportunity to observe many things that others don't. One day in eighth grade language arts class, we were talking about dependent and independent clauses along with coordinating conjunctions, affectionately referred to as FANBOYS(for, and, neither, but, or, yet and so).The very next day at high school in eleventh-grade communication arts, we were talking about the same thing.I don't understand this.Was the eleventh-grade teacher just reviewing?Where in the curriculum is this to be taught? No wonder the students seem bored; they have done this before at least once, but I am willing to bet even more. I do believe that part of the repetition occurs because all juniors in the high school where I teach take the ACT, facilitated by our high school. A large portion of the test focuses on grammar and punctuation.

Columbia scholar Lauren Resnick has argued that one of the key features of programs that teach thinking, learning, or higher-order cognitive skills is that they are organized around the joint accomplishment of tasks, so the elements of the skill take on meaning in the context of the whole (Schwarz 2005 as cited by Weber 2010).One of the teachers I work with does a great job of breaking up the parts of an essay into smaller chunks.When the students complete all the smaller chunks, they put them together to make a complete essay without feeling overwhelmed.The students feel proud of themselves at the paper's completion because they had written an entire paper when most didn't think they could.Faced with writing in the future, they will feel confident in their abilities.

Students want a great education but are aware they are not always receiving it. When we offer a great education to them, they will go after it with everything they have (Rhee 1997 as cited by Weber 2010). When students even just begin to get what they need from their schools, they begin to drive change and hold themselves to high expectations (Rhee 1997 as cited by Weber 2010). Schools that succeed are built on collaborative, trusting relationships. These schools create environments where ordinary, devoted people can work together to achieve extraordinary things on behalf of students (Weingarten 2010).

So, here's part of the problem. Not all teachers are great teachers. I believe that some teachers, whether it be intentional or unintentional, provoke kids. An example: a student who had difficulties dealing with stress when feeling overwhelmed had administrative permission to put his hood up and retreat, much like a turtle does. I can only think of one reason why a teacher would continue to go at this student, insisting he take his hood down. This bullying by a person who is supposed to protect him is never acceptable. This certainly does not create a relationship with this student. The student was quietly and non-disruptively using his coping strategy to deal with stress, and the teacher continued creating stress.

One of my colleagues in the special education department, working specifically with students with behavior issues, asked me if I thought some teachers would intentionally set our kids up. I answered with a strong, “They do.” She continued questioning me as to whether something should be said to this teacher. After thinking for a minute, I said, “ Yes. I would suggest you tell that teacher you are aware that “Ben” is doing some things in class that you don’t appreciate. Please write down those things for me , and I will address them with him. This way you are not taking class time to deal with this, but that it will be taken care of. Then you, as the special education teacher, can share the concerns with “Ben” however you feel best, at an appropriate time, and probably more gently.

Now the regular education teacher feels heard and supported and the relationship between the teacher and "Ben" is saved a little bit." I'm not sure if all teachers set kids up intentionally or if it is unintentional. Hopefully, it is the latter. Again, we must know our students.

As assistant principal at the high school I supervised a teacher at the high school. He was so good at making relationships with students and was a decent teacher. He would refer to students by name, find out what they liked, and incorporate that into his lessons. However, he wasn't always where he was supposed to be or was sometimes late for school; but he believed bringing doughnuts would excuse him for being late. Because he didn't have all the required components of a great teacher, he could never become one. Dealing with this is an administrative problem, so I'll address this more in the next section.

It is very irritating, however, for great teachers who know the person in the next room is getting paid the same for being mediocre. Great teachers do not have it in their DNA to slack even though they would like to at times, based on the previous comment. Great teachers need to realize they are the glue that holds the school together and they should feel empowered by this knowledge. With that status and knowledge comes an implied responsibility to alert the administration of the shortcomings of your fellow teachers. I know you don't feel like this is part of your job, but if your commitment is to your students and providing them the best possible education from the school you call home, it is everyone's responsibility. A typical school has eighty teachers and maybe three administrators. Based on the law of averages alone, it makes sense you know more about your fellow teachers than the administration. Your responsibility stops at reporting your fellow "slackers" to the administration who should take it from here. You should not feel bad about this. Two things should happen after you report this information; one, after speaking with the administration, the slacking teacher puts more effort into their teaching and reinvents themselves into the great teacher they can be; or two, they are relieved of their duties because they are not good for student learning. It really should be that simple. If you are not part of the solution, you are part of the problem. If you truly want the best for your students, you must step up. I shared earlier how teachers should approach their administrators.

Many secondary schools are on block scheduling and although this may be more like a college setting, I don't believe it is best for students. I feel that students would have higher retention rates if they saw their teachers daily. I'm not convinced all teachers have been properly trained in teaching in a block schedule and therefore time is wasted. I also think that a seven-period day that has a shorter amount of time, makes it easier for teachers to hold the students' attention. The learning would be in smaller chunks and delivered more frequently. For schools that are currently on block schedules, returning to a seven-period day also requires fewer teachers, potentially saving the district money.

I would be willing to bet that at least 90% of the teachers who leave education in the first few years are due to discipline issues within their classrooms. We all wonder what has happened with the respect given to all adults. Teachers used to be viewed as someone to respect and revere. While on plan, a colleague of mine recently went into the restroom at the high school. Several girls were in there and the bell had already rung for class to start. She said, "Girls, the bell already rang. You should hurry to class." One of the girls questioned her as to who she was. Her response was, "I'm an adult!" When and how did questioning a school authority become ok? You are not going to like this, but it is mostly our fault! Teachers in general do not hold students consistently accountable especially when it comes to discipline. It is harder than ever with the incorporation of electronics into education. There are many good reasons that electronics should be in education. However, teachers need to reclaim their classrooms. Cell phones are an addiction for many teenagers and a nationwide problem. Some schools have tackled the problem head-on, banning cell phones during instructional hours of school unless the teacher asks the students to use them for classroom purposes. Banning cell phones requires everyone working together in the school to make this achievable. A chain is only as strong as the weakest link, and it only takes one person to cave in and not follow the expectations of the building! No one wants to be the bad guy, but it helps everyone if you do your part by standing your ground. For the past eight years, schools in 41 states and 21 countries have spent millions of dollars on magnetic pouches that are used to lock up cell phones to limit use during school hours. The most popular pouches are produced by a company called Yondr. Their pouch has created the possibility of a phone free school district. In 2023, education saw a 150% increase of schools using the pouch, but at what costs? Each pouch costs districts between $25-$30 per student (Mather 2024). In a school with 1000 students, that is $25000-$30000 for magnetic bags so students stop using their cell phones during instructional time. I can think of so many more meaningful ways to spend this money. Shouldn't schools and parents working together be able to address this problem without spending money that could be used for educational purposes? In my current middle school, phones are not allowed out during the day or they are taken to the office. The students and parents have adjusted, and it has worked very well. It can be done without these magnetic pouches. Other schools have taken a more individual approach and left it up to teachers and their classrooms. This is a cop-out by the administration who need to do the right thing, support their teachers, and do what is best for student learning. If your administrator isn't going to take the heat off you by enacting a no-phone policy, then the teacher will have to do it yourself. Make it known that phones are not to be seen until permitted by the teacher: no laptops opened, no earbuds, or headphones in without approval from the teacher. Explain to the students why you have these rules: number one, it is rude for students to be on electronics when you are teaching; and number two, electronics interfere with your ability to teach. Lay out the consequences for failure to follow your rules. It would be a simple insubordination infraction that they were not doing as instructed by the teacher. FOLLOW THROUGH! The only person you are hurting is you if you don't! You will never have credibility again and you can kiss discipline goodbye if you don't. It is hard the first few times but then it becomes a habit. Of course, students will say you are the only one that does this and it's not fair. Your response should be something to the effect that they are lucky you care enough about them to be the best teacher you can be. Hold students accountable. Most students want parameters or boundaries.

Regarding students seeing teachers as role models and trusting adults, my hope was renewed a little the other day. I had placed an order for $2.82 at a local fast food place. As I pulled up to the window, the cashier was one of my former students whom I knew very well. We said "hi" as I handed her $20.82, but then she called for help because she had accidentally typed in $2.82. The girl who came to help her said to me, "Can you do that in your head?"

I responded , "Yes, I will receive $18.00 back because the change was exact." My former student responded, "You can trust her, she is a teacher." She handed me my $18 and I left with a smile on my face, feeling that maybe in a small way I had made an impact on her life and she trusted me.

Beginning in the 2024-2025 school year, two of the largest school districts in the United States–New York and Los Angeles–are not allowing students to have cell phones during the school day. I believe this is a step in the right direction and puts classrooms back in teachers' hands, unlike the mandate for the Ten Commandments and the teaching of the Bible in Louisiana and Oklahoma.

Do not be afraid to ask for help from other teachers or administration if you are struggling with a particular student and behavior. There is a high probability that if you are experiencing problems with this student, other teachers struggle with them as well and may be able to offer advice on what worked for them. If you do not seek help, this one student could make your life miserable. Administrators do not see asking for help as a weakness but as a sign of being proactive and problem-solving.

Recently as we were reviewing for a test, a young lady was on her phone. I went up to her and quietly asked her to get off her phone. At the beginning of class I had announced aloud for everyone to hear that no one should be on their phone. This is not a new expectation, but a daily one. Since she was still on her phone, I walked over and quietly said again, "You must put your phone up or you'll have to put it at the front of the room." She responded, "I'm not putting anything upfront, and you need to get the hell away from me." I told her to go to the office, which she refused to do. I called the office for an administrator, but she eventually left the class on her own. I'm not sure what was going on with her, but she was angry and not at me still I had to hold her accountable.

If students are disrupting your class by constantly talking or making noises, first try proximity, (moving closer to the student); second, make continuous eye contact after they see you, and then continue for about fifteen seconds or until they look up a second time. This way they know that you mean business. As a last option,calmly remind students of the classroom rules and ask if they can follow them. Do this quietly and individually. Most of the time, they will say they can and then remind them they weren't. Do not try to embarrass the student in front of the class.

If none of this works, send the student out to a buddy room. If this behavior repeats the next time you see them, go through the same progression. Then call home and let parents know that the next time there will be an office referral. Do not be afraid of parents. Discipline must be established early on and must be consistent. It is not fair to all the other students who are wanting to learn, as they are losing instructional time because of a disruptive student. Do not believe you are weak, or your administrator thinks you are weak, because you write referrals. They will see you are controlling your classroom and maximizing learning opportunities.

In my early days as a coach, while in our team huddle, at the end of practice before the next day's game, we decided to dress up for school. Two of the girls on my freshman team decided they didn't want to dress up. Both girls typically saw a lot of playing time; in fact, one was my starting point guard. I easily could have turned a blind eye, saying that if this ever happened again, there would be consequences. But what is right is not always popular and what is popular is not always right. I contacted both girls' parents, explained what they had done, and shared their punishment: they would not play that night nor wear the uniform.. I honestly can't tell you how the game turned out, but I clearly remember the incident. I was talking to the mother of one of the young ladies the other day, and she said that their family still talks about this and how their daughter was held accountable. I remember how tough this was for me to follow through, but it was the right decision.

When I interviewed for the elementary principal position, I recall them asking me if I liked conflict. I remember saying, "I did not necessarily like it, but I was not afraid of it." Truth is I am an empath, so each time I must impose discipline on someone or have a tough conversation it eats at me. I feel what they feel!

At the elementary, if I was called to a teacher's classroom because a student wouldn't leave when asked to by the teacher, I would usually walk up to the student slowly and quietly whisper in their ear, "I don't want to embarrass you in front of your friends, so why don't you just get up and walk out of here with me." I would guess that 90% of the time this worked. It was a win-win, the troubled student saved face in front of the class, and the teacher got what they wanted. Because I was in the classrooms every day, several times a day, my initial coming into the room didn't put anyone on alert for fight or flight.

Being an educator comes with many more duties than educating students. Teachers have supervisory duties before and after school. Dance, hallway, and assembly supervision are all part of the job. Most teachers do this because it is what is expected of them, and they realize the importance.Those who don't follow the rules leave room for safety issues to occur. These teachers should be reprimanded because others are having to cover for them. Lack of supervision in these areas can lead to fights and the chance of someone getting hurt, and frankly could put everyone in danger.

At the high school at the end of the day, a fight broke out in an area that I typically wasn't. One of the students I teach yelled, "Ms. Reynolds, there is a fight!" I went to the area as quickly as I could, weaving through the students already gathered and taking videos. As a side note, when fights occur in middle and high school, it is common for students to gather and take videos on their phones to post on social media. I believe these students videoing are as guilty as the students fighting and should be disciplined. When I got to the fight, two paraprofessionals were already involved in breaking up the fight, so I just assisted them. After reflecting on this and checking facts, I realized the fight could have been averted had the teacher responsible for supervising his students was where he should have been. One of the students involved in the fight had a knife, so the outcome could have been much worse had the paras not arrived so quickly. One of them later shared with me she had been involved with helping break up a fight last year when she had gotten hurt. This same teacher who dropped the ball at this current fight, had also dropped the ball back then, stood back, and did nothing to help her as she was getting assaulted. This is unacceptable and speaks to the importance of being in your assigned area.Hopefully, this teacher was disciplined for not doing his job.

We all remember the tragic school shooting in Uvalde, Texas, that May 24, 2022. The gunman entered through a door that a teacher didn't fully close after retrieving some supplies from her car. She did attempt to close the door after she removed the rock that she had previously placed in the door jam. Unfortunately, the door was supposed to latch and lock when she pulled it shut, but it didn't operate properly, thus allowing the shooter to enter. The teacher only pulled the rock out of the door when she knew there was an intruder. I feel terrible for everyone who died that day, the families of those victims, and for the teacher who the door malfunctioned for. I cannot imagine the guilt and pain she carries with her each day. The rock should never have been placed in the door under any circumstances. Safety protocols are established for a reason, and these protocols must be followed by everyone.

In Tennessee, the House just passed a bill to allow some trained teachers and staff to carry handguns. It is currently being sent to the governor. The armed teachers, who will be required to undergo training, will be allowed to carry handguns in their classrooms and on most campuses' without informing parents or colleagues that they're armed. Before the bill was sent to the governor, several attempts to amend the bill were rejected. Some of the rejected amendments suggested were: requiring teachers to keep their handguns locked up during school unless there was a security breach; holding teachers civilly liable for using their handgun on campus; and informing parents when guns are on campus. Some arguments for allowing armed classroom teachers include: to protect students as a deterrent for potential school safety threats; and to increase school security, particularly in rural areas where there exists a greater response time by emergency personnel. Some of those loudest opponents for not allowing guns in schools came from parents of school shooting survivors. Some of these parents point out their children were saved when teachers kept their students quiet and out of sight. Another parent shared that because of gaps in training and the extra burden placed on teachers trained to carry guns, they were being set up for failure. Others cite the secrecy clause in the bill, which bars school administrators from revealing who in the school is armed(Brown and Latham 2024). I in no way see this as a possible solution to school shootings. I cannot imagine placing more guns in school could make it safer. Also teachers are just people and frustration does occur with students at school. I have known a few teachers who when frustrated, might let students know they had a gun. There are so many ways this would not be safe. Students could legitimately be scared of the teacher, a student may try to physically challenge the armed teacher, or a student might bring a gun to school to retaliate against the teacher. This certainly does not jive with most schools' themes of warm and welcoming.

Everyone involved with schools needs to take every aspect of safety seriously. Last year I kicked out a rock that had been placed in the door by a middle school teacher because she had gone to her car to make a phone call. This lazy and selfish act puts everyone at risk. All school district employees have keys or key fobs.

Here is another example of teachers not doing their jobs, not working together, or having each other's back: Two students were fighting in a middle school hallway. A male and female teacher jumped in to stop them. By chance, the female teacher grabbed the more aggressive student while the male teacher controlled the other. The female teacher took hits to the face and was having difficulty controlling that student. A new teacher, who was male, stood at his door, watched this all happen, and did nothing. Maybe he can be excused because he is new, but shouldn't it be common sense to help another adult/ fellow teacher? Today the female teacher harbors resentment toward her grade level team member. She knows this is not a good thing and that she needs to work through it for team cohesiveness. Incidentally, the female teacher had to go to court to testify about what happened and her being assaulted. Often, a teacher's day does not end at 3:30. As you can see, it is not only about teaching subject matter; a teacher's job is all encompassing.

Educators cannot possibly do everything by themselves; it truly does take a village. Paraprofessionals are a godsend. Most of them who I have worked with are paired with some of the most difficult students for little pay. They are versed in many subjects and keep detailed classroom notes so substitutes can help the students if the para ever misses a day, which they rarely do. Paraprofessionals are the unsung heroes in any school. As you can see by the example I shared about the recent fight at the high school and how they reacted, they are selfless and put student safety above all.

If a teacher has been teaching for a long time, they may not need to have extremely detailed lesson plans for each hour of each day because they know the material to be presented and how it is to be presented. When a substitute is required in a classroom, detailed lesson plans need to be available. This is a case where more is better. Have you ever wondered why great teachers don't like to miss school? It is because lesson plans for a substitute take a long time to write. It is almost more work to write lesson plans than it is just to come to work and teach. Make sure good substitute lesson plans are always readily available. Good substitutes are hard to come by and if good lesson plans are not left, they will not return, making it more difficult for all of us. Remember, teachers often must cover other teachers' classrooms during their plan if there is no substitute available and they too need plans to go by.

When my dad passed away, I was a teacher at the high school. I was devastated and missed about three weeks of school. The substitute and I worked together to ensure lessons and learning continued as if I were there. She did an amazing job.

Teachers must be heard when they voice inequities in education. They must not settle for low pay. There is strength in numbers, and **you must remember your worth.** Teachers touch everyone and are the ones who create all other professions.

Summary

Teachers are the most important ingredient in everyone's educational journey. Great teachers must be in every school. Educators should be paid like the professionals they are, with starting salaries in the $50,000-$60,000 range. With the salary increase should come extra hours are needed for reteaching, enrichment, and acceleration.

Educators need to be comfortable speaking to the administration about team members who are not carrying their weight. They must remember that their loyalty and commitment is to the students.

Schools should run year-round to maintain as much retention as possible. There should be as many subsequent breaks as possible throughout the year to equal that of what the summer break would be.

Teachers must teach students how to ask and answer questions and see another person's perspective. Perhaps if we can learn to communicate and tolerate one another, the number of fights and shootings will decrease. Hopefully the world can begin to heal and become kinder and more understanding.

Educators must establish classroom rules and consistently follow these rules. Lack of discipline is one of the biggest reasons teachers leave the profession within the first few years.

Teach each student as the individual learner they are. There are no one-size-fits-all lessons. Everyone's brain is wired differently.

Relationships must be formed between teachers and their students, so students feel comfortable sharing ideas and asking questions when they do not understand. Tracking would help with the comfort of students asking questions and contributing to discussions.

We must appreciate all employees in the building and let them know how important they are. It takes all of us working together to make the best possible learning experience for our students.

All adults need to step up and behave like respectable citizens and model what it looks like when you disagree with someone. It doesn't look like violence or name-calling. The world must change by accepting and tolerating differences in people and ideas. Historically change has occurred through peaceful protest.

Considerations for Administrators

"An education system isn't truly successful until all children-regardless of background and resources-have the opportunity to reach their full potential"(Grant 254). A leader's worth is reflected in their team's growth, not their spotlight (Leadership Lines). First and foremost, empower all people in the building/district and let them know how valuable they are to you and the community. Continue praising them periodically showing them appreciation. This gesture, no matter how small, will go far in building and maintaining relationships and retaining staff. Until evidence proves differently, administrators must always be supportive of their teachers, nurses, custodians, counselors, social workers, secretaries, and building administrators. Trust the people you have in all positions and do not try to micromanage.I can't tell you how many times as the building administrator I stepped in to stop an upset parent verbally abusive or belittling one of the building personnel. More than anything employees must believe you have their backs. They need to understand they are an important part of your team and they are important to you. Simple gestures, like stepping into a teacher's classroom and inviting them to take fifteen minutes because you have their class, will go a long way. Everyone in schools loves drinks and chocolate, so bringing these items or any kind of food is a great boost for all.

All support staff are extremely important to administrators, teachers,and students alike. Custodians can be your best friend and can be friends with students as well; show them your appreciation. I was lucky enough to hear Joe Sanfelippo speak at a district in-service in the fall of 2023. Joe shared that he took his custodian's job for the day. He said he told everyone they couldn't throw up because if he had to clean it up, he too would throw up. He remarked on the importance of his custodian. Because the students all knew Joe, he shared with them how difficult "Wanda's" job was at the school, and when she returned the next day, all the students called her by name and thanked her. What a simple gesture to do for someone making them feel part of the team and appreciated.

Great school nursers are loved by all and should be treasured. They deal with all kinds of medical issues and bodily fluids most of us cannot handle. They not only take care of students but the adults in the buildings as well. As with many people working in schools, they could make more money working outside of education, but stay because they love students.

Social workers conference with students who may not smell very well and offer them clean clothes to wear. Not all schools are blessed to have social workers as part of their staff but if you do, consider yourself very fortunate. Social workers pair with agencies to help families receive services they may not have known were available. Social workers provide transportation to individuals when needed and many more services.

School counselors not only prepare student schedules but provide counsel to students and faculty alike. Their jobs have been more stressful and busier since COVID-19. School counselors, social workers, and school nurses all work together to help anyone struggling within our schools.

We all are aware who really runs the school. A school secretary can set the mood of a building since they are often the first person seen by those entering the building. Secretaries can be trusted with confidential information and know everything going on in the school.

Imagine how grumpy everyone would be if we weren't fed at school. Cooks and kitchen staff often have great relationships with students because they see most students at least once a day and are providing a service everyone is interested in, food.

Not all public schools are blessed with leaders who recognize the importance of the school-community bond. Super schools need super leaders and finding the right leader for a building or a district is of utmost importance. A great leader demonstrates the ability to teach and love children, demonstrate positive people skills, and the ability to be tough when necessary. Effective leaders are often very emotionally intelligent. These leaders must be self-aware and able to view things objectively and possess the power to hire and fire teachers without interference from unions, the board of education, or any other entity (Matthews 2010 as cited by Weber 2010). The right leader must be given the administrative freedom and independence to make rapid situational decisions and the resource base needed to support what they have chosen (Strickland 1971 as cited by Weber 2010).

Administrators who cannot think on their feet in times of crisis, those without a vision, and those who cannot see their schools future are not good leaders.

Anyone wanting to pursue administration should be a teacher first for at least seven years. Someone becoming an administrator without teaching experience first will not have the confidence of their staff. You must have walked in their shoes to be able to fully understand the situation to offer credible advice. Lazy administrators, like lazy teachers, have no place leading a building. Just as great teachers are important to the success of a school, an ineffective administrator can destroy a building in a relatively short period. Just because you can, doesn’t mean you should. I have witnessed many great athletes who have tried to transition to coaching and they were ineffective. Some great teachers just do not have what it takes to be an administrator and that's okay.

When I was still a high school teacher, I had to go to the bathroom so bad I was just holding on until the bell rang so I could get to the closest restroom. Three-two-one bell. The closest restroom was located in the main office,only two single restrooms directly across from each other . I walked as fast as I could to the office, rounded the corner to the restrooms, and there in between the two restrooms stood my principal and a math teacher talking. I stopped for just a second and tried to wait patiently ,but knew I couldn't afford to wait. I said, "excuse me" and ducked between and under them into a restroom. As I was closing the door, the principal condescendingly said ,"This is not a faculty restroom!" to which I replied, "It is if I'm about to go in my pants!" And with that, I closed the door. As I'm in the restroom I'm thinking, I just barked at my principal. He is wrong though because it is a faculty restroom, all of us use it daily. What if they are still there talking when I open the door? What will I say? When I opened the door, thank heavens they were gone. The math teacher found me and said the principal was out of line and he was sorry he had acted that way. The principal's secretary called me that night because she had heard what was said. She was crying because she felt so bad about how I was treated. A couple of days passed, and the principal found me. He tried to apologize but there was a "but" involved, so he just could not admit he was wrong. He was not a good principal. He tried to run the building through fear. The story I just shared is nothing compared to what he did to other staff members.

I have worked with four administrators who were good people and cared about kids, but they were not leaders and were nothing more than mere placeholders. I have been blessed to work with four great administrators who were able to keep everything balanced and the building ran smoothly. These administrators established a safe environment for students and staff, had a vision and expectations for all, demanded respect and the following of rules. If rules were not followed, conversations were had and reprimands were made.

Individuals with proven skills in innovation, entrepreneurship, business management are inspirational leaders. Potential candidates could be drawn from industry, universities, community organizations, and non-profit organizations (Strickland 1971 as cited by Weber 2010). Giving power and responsibility to school administrators and teachers means a shift in how we think about school management because creating and maintaining a strong, functional, and progressive educational system begins at the top. We must loosen the traditional bureaucratic political and union rules necessary to bring our schools into the 21st century. Change can be challenging for all stakeholders including parents, the board of education, and unions, but the alternative path leads to continued failure, which is not an acceptable option (Strickland 1971 as cited by Weber 2010). I would recommend that a new administrator coming into a district or building does not change too much in the first year. You must take time to assess the current system and evaluate what is working, and what is not. You fit your initiative to your personnel, not your personnel to your initiative. Prioritize, and if there is a better or more efficient way to do things do not retain the old ways because traditionally it has been done that way. Some things should be done immediately. The summer before I started as principal at the elementary school, I developed a faculty handbook that contained important dates for faculty meetings and emergency procedure drills, as well as teacher expectations. I'm not sure how anyone knew what they were supposed to do before this handbook was established.

Once we have the right leader(s) in place, we can begin to look at the problem with teachers, too few and not enough good ones. The quality of a teacher is best judged by performance in the classroom reflected by students' gains in learning. Building-level administrators should strive to be in teachers' classrooms at least once a day. This accomplishes two goals: the teacher knows that you will be coming in at some point, this holds them accountable and lets them know you truly care, and this also allows you to know what is or isn't happening in the classrooms. You need to be visible so students know who you are. District-level administrators must try to visit buildings at least once a month so they do not get too far removed from the educational process , support the teachers, and gain a pulse for the building.

An assistant principal in Virginia who did not listen to her teachers or have their backs has been charged with eight counts of felony child abuse and disregard for life after a teacher in her building was shot in the hand and chest by a six year old boy.

Abigail Zwerner filed a lawsuit in April 2023, after warning her assistant principal; the assistant principal failed to take action to prevent the shooting. According to an article published in USA Today, April 9, 2024, Zwerner alleged that she visited her assistant principal's office hours before the shooting, informing her the boy seemed more off than usual. Zwerner told Parker, her assistant principal, the boy had already threatened to beat up another student. Less than an hour later another teacher allegedly told Parker that other students had reported this same boy had a gun in his backpack. It is reported that yet another teacher told Parker that the boy had a gun in his pocket and again nothing was done. Parker resigned from her position after the shooting (Mayes-Osterman). Zwerner quit teaching as well. Trust your staff and follow- up on what they share with you. We can't afford to lose more good educators.

Many school districts do not have enough teachers to instruct all their classes, and some schools that do have enough teachers don't have quality teachers Standard policies do not ensure that quality teachers are recruited or retained in the profession. Finding solutions to this problem is of utmost importance given the rate of teacher retirement, the lack of people going into the field of education, and the huge number of teachers who must be hired over the next few years.

Without some significant changes in the current ineffective system for hiring and training teachers, the hope of improving student outcomes is small. If teacher certification requirements end up discouraging potentially high-quality teachers who do not want to take the specific required or can't afford the classes, the requirements then appear more like a ceiling instead of a floor. (Hanushek 2009 as cited by Weber 2010).

As discussed earlier, teacher performance matters significantly and ineffective teachers should be removed from the classroom. The leader of each building along with the director of personnel should be included in these decisions. Those many skilled and dedicated teachers already at work in our schools need resources, training, rewards, and encouragement to continue and improve their efforts (Weber 9).

A strong leader must be willing to hire a long-term substitute with special skills, rather than leave a teacher who is ineffective in the classroom (Matthews 2010 as cited by Weber 2010). The needs of students should take precedence over the job security of the small number of teachers who should not be in the classroom.

Eric Hanushek from Stanford University states, " If we could just eliminate the bottom six to ten percent of our teachers and replace them with just an average teacher, we could bring the average United States student up to the top of the world today." We must reward schools and teachers who promote high achievement and not reward those who fail. Great teachers will appreciate the recognition and will also appreciate those who are not doing their jobs being replaced.

Looking at the range of quality for teachers within a single large urban district, teachers near the top of the quality distribution can garner an entire year's worth of additional learning from their students compared to those near the bottom. In a single academic year, a good teacher will gain one and one-half grade-level equivalents, while a bad teacher will gain equivalents to just half a year (Hanushek 2009 as cited by Weber 2010). The only way to ensure a student is placed with a high-quality teacher is to **employ** all high-quality teachers; otherwise, a student could have poor teachers for three years in a row with three years' worth of potential achievement loss.

When hiring teachers and staff, we want well-trained teachers who hold themselves accountable for their students' success. We must focus on everybody's contribution to learning ,and we need to hold all accountable for the learning gains they do or do not produce. We need to decentralize decision-making so local schools -where demands are known, where people are known, and where programs can be designed to increase achievement have the freedom to perform (Hanushek 2009 as cited by Weber 2010).

Even though more money has been invested into education, with nationwide 2020-2021 per pupil expenditure around $15000, United States' reading and math scores have remained relatively flat. Although, these scores have risen in virtually every other developed country (NEA Rankings and Estimates 2023).

If we look around the world, countries with high educational achievement also have high rates of economic growth. This relationship is especially important to our future as a nation because economic growth is what provides us with increasing incomes and greater economic well-being over time. (Hanushek 2009 as cited by Weber 2010). As mentioned earlier, the United States isn't performing up to the educational standards of many other countries. If this can't be rectified our future economic success will be negatively affected.

In 2020, 123 million high-paying, high-skilled jobs in occupations from computer programming to bioengineering were needed, but only fifty million Americans were qualified to fill them. The economy requires a higher percentage of college graduates. The gap between what we need and what we have is large (Gates 2009 as cited by Weber 2010).

Districts face a huge problem and must be very creative when trying to recruit and retain great teachers. One of the most enticing incentives to offer teachers is higher pay. It is not that most districts don't want to pay teachers 'more, but it is simply not in the budget. However, when a teacher can go to work making twenty dollars an hour, work a forty-hour week, and bring home about the same as a beginning teacher, schools struggle to compete with this. The job I just discussed might not offer health insurance, which is often provided by school districts. Retirement benefits are part of teaching but might not be a benefit provided by another employer outside of education. Education retirement benefits are very good if you can make it thirty years. Missouri has one of the best retirement programs in the nation. Often though when you are just trying to keep food on the table, many of these benefits are overlooked, especially by young adults just entering the world of work. Also, at another job outside of education, you would not be burdened with after-school duties, grading papers, and meeting academic targets; you just go home when the day is over.

Missouri lawmakers have proposed hikes in teacher salaries and benefits, but they have yet to pass. Arkansas, Missouri's neighbor, just passed legislation in July 2023, to increase starting teacher salaries to $50,000 (Hanshaw 2024). I believe this is a step in the right direction. As of May 20, 2024, Governor Mike Parsons of Missouri, signed senate bill 727 into law . The bill has a large number of components, but here are some of the aspects that will affect districts the most: minimum teacher salary increased to $40,000 starting in 2025-26, $41K in 2026-27, $42K in 2027-28, and then increases annually with inflation at a three percent cap;

districts should see an increase in funding per student as the calculation will no longer be solely based on attendance; the teacher baseline salary grant will continue to support districts to get up to the minimum; districts could see an increase in funding based on pre-school enrollment; and bonus payment for 5-day school week districts. If a school district maintains a 5 -day school week years 2025-26 and 2026-27, the district will receive a 1% bonus in formula payment but only if the calendar has a minimum of 169 days. In 2027-28, the bonus increases to 2%, and these bonus payments must be expended on teacher salaries. The current projection is around $150,000 for two years, then increasing to over $300,000 in 2027-28. This could be a game changer for many districts, especially smaller ones.

According to Bill and Melinda Gates in Educating America's Young People for the Global Economy in 2009, "America spends about eight billion a year to reward teachers who have earned a master's degree, even though some evidence says in most cases a teacher's master's degree does nothing to improve student achievement. Our nation is spending billions funding salary schedules based on a seniority system, even though the evidence says that after the first five years, seniority does not impact student achievement. We've also spent billions to reduce class size in high schools even though there is no strong evidence that this improves student performance (Weber 2010)." I do believe that smaller class sizes in elementary schools do make a measurable difference as students are trying to master basic skills.

When it comes to specific topics of public schools, the sense of cynicism and hopelessness is widespread. For the most part, people recognize the difficulties facing education, but they face the problem with a sense of helplessness. Rather than looking for ways to help, they tend to hide their heads in the sand believing there is nothing that they can do. C. S. Lewis once said, "One of the most cowardly things ordinary people do is to shut their eyes to facts." Sadly, they believe that somehow if they ignore the problem, it will go away. This is not working!

Students thrive when their schools encourage positive learning relationships among families, educators, faith groups, civic organizations, businesses, and other members of the community. Parents should have opportunities to visit the school building, talk with teachers and staff, voice concerns, share ideas, serve as volunteers, and suggest ways to improve the school. School leaders should reach out to their neighborhoods by attending community events and forming partnerships with local organizations to increase effectiveness and tap into additional resources (The Alliance for Excellent Education).

The time we remove fear and defeat from the vocabulary of the schools in our communities is **now.** The ultimate price we pay for a failed school is the loss of hope for present and future generations- a price we simply can't afford to pay any longer (Strickland 1971 as cited by Weber 2010).

The era of schools and educators talking only to themselves must come to an end. No system, no matter how innovative, will survive in the modern world by closing itself off to good ideas from a variety of sources (Strickland 1971 as cited by Weber 2010). The sooner everyone acknowledges this, the sooner we can begin to solve the problem.

Most public schools are reluctant to forge links with businesses. If failing schools were willing to take a critical look at their circumstances and ask for help in rebranding themselves, I believe most industry leaders would respond to the call without hesitation (Strickland 1971 as cited by Weber 2010). However, some administrators feel this requires admitting you can't do the job for which you were hired. Ego's need to be set aside and it should be remembered that everyone needs help at one time or another. Are schools/administrators afraid that if they open the door for help, they will lose too much control ?

There is an untapped resource in educational reform, and it is the average citizen from all walks of life. More than any new curriculum, new funding source, or new management plan, what students need is more attention, love, good teaching, and guidance from more adults. Qualified members of our communities need to pitch- in… "citizen teachers", architects, chefs,engineers,filmmakers, and other professionals… who could partner with classroom teachers to teach students their expertise (Schwarz 2006 as cited by Weber 2010). Years ago while teaching high school, I asked students what their plans were after graduation. One of the students wanted to work in the movie industry behind the scenes. Another student dreamed of being a rapper. After doing some research and talking to several people, I was able to secure a producer who worked on the Superman franchise and a rapper recording artist to visit my classroom, share their experiences, answer questions, and offer advice to each of these students. Incidentally, both of these gentlemen were Warrensburg High School graduates from Warrensburg, Missouri. I realize that is not an option every time and at every school. You never know until you try and just ask the question. Schools should consider industry and the business world as important sources of faculty to conduct core courses (Strickland 1971 as cited by Weber 2010). We encourage creativity in our students in the United States and yet we don't encourage creativity in how we run our schools (Chilcott 2010 as cited by Weber 2010). What if we invite different adults to teach in different ways at different times during a student's day? Essentially, this could create a second shift that gives students vastly expanded opportunities to learn, grow, and make those important connections. By broadening the definition of "teacher," such a program would make it possible to tailor daily lessons and activities to individual students' strengths, weaknesses, and interests. This model focuses on high expectations for all students while freeing them to learn in different ways at their own pace. Adding more adults to the mix makes it all possible (Schwartz 2006 as cited by Weber 2010). These extra teachers are not replacing regular teachers but enhancing and extending learning.

When I first retired, I obtained my insurance license and worked at State Farm for a time. My boss, at the State Farm office, graduated from UCM with a degree in marketing. When the university found itself without a marketing teacher, they reached out to her to instruct students at UCM. She did not have teacher certification but did such a great job, they asked her to continue. If universities can expand their faculty this way, why can't it be done in grades K-12?

There is evidence to suggest that schools with volunteers do better because of the **3 R's:** more **R**elationships, more **R**elevant learning projects, and more time for **R**igorous practice and skill building. But sociologist Robert Putnam says, "These schools are successful for additional reasons: they have more of what he calls 'social capital,' the web of mutual commitments and networks among citizens who know one another." In Putnam's book *Bowling Alone,* he states that social capital has a significantly larger impact on student performance than does overall school spending, parent income, or parent education levels (6). By engaging parents and other adult volunteers in a school community, create a support system that reinforces and builds upon the work of teachers and overcomes the challenges of poverty (Schwartz 2006 as cited by Weber 2010).

America has met its biggest challenges when its citizens become directly involved.All our children need and deserve networks of adults who see their full potential and are dedicated to helping them succeed. Now at this moment of urgency, it is time to open the schoolhouse doors wide to welcome in new talent and fresh thinking (Schwartz 2006 as cited by Weber 2010).

Part of my current job at the high school is to find businesses within the community that will accept student workers. There they will gain work experience and be exposed to many different types of jobs. As a result, they might find a job they enjoy and excel at. Pursuing businesses requires a lot of door-knocking, but once managers agree, they do a remarkable job explaining to the students what needs to be accomplished, working with the students to model tasks, and making good connections with them. Business leaders are very accommodating; all we must do is ask. Another positive aspect of this program allows students to be visible in the community. I always share with my students that many times it is not how much you know, but who you know that gets your foot in the door.

I worked several hours and had several meetings with a large employer in our city who had contacted me to include my students in job shadowing experiences. I believed some of my students could do what would be required of them. I was very excited about this opportunity because it had benefits and an hourly rate almost double that of the minimum wage. This would change many of their lives. We had worked through everything, so I thought. When I completed the parent letter explaining what the students would be doing, I asked my principal to look it over. He took it to Central Office for final approval. My letter was fine but because students had the slight possibility of lead exposure, the district wouldn't take the risk even if parents signed the permission letter. Of course, I don't want to hurt my students in any way, but it was a little disappointing. The bottom line, businesses are willing to work with schools and are excited about the possibility of doing so.

Successful schools have a constant focus on gathering real information about student performance early and often, using that data to have a much more drilled-down look at a student's ability, then creating an action plan to target an individual student's deficiencies. The ability to collect, use, and interpret data is an ongoing way many successful schools use consistently (Canada 1997 as cited by Weber 2010).

Let's focus on hiring great teachers first instead of hiring coaches and hoping they can teach. I understand many students don't necessarily like school and only tolerate it because of athletics, but our job is to educate. I also realize and understand that many important life lessons are learned through athletics.

Perhaps not the state standards, but important lessons such as functioning within a team. However, we are preparing students for the future, and only a small fraction of them will be able to support themselves through athletics. Most cities have parks and recreation programs,as well as traveling teams and sports clubs available for students to join. Athletics has been an important part of my life and I hold a physical education degree . I realize the benefits of athletics, but if education and improving our status in the world is our focus, let's remove distractions like European countries do. Athletics should be an enhancement to academics, not an equal part. Removing expenditures for coaches, facilities, equipment, and out of town transportation would save the district money. If the community resists ending athletics, perhaps scheduling morning practices for those involved would allow more time for after school academics. Another option might be a specifically designed physical education class devoted to athletes so they could practice during school hours.

One way to enable districts to retain teachers would be to establish a four-day workweek. Out of the 567 school districts in Missouri, 168 have adopted four-day work weeks. This has been an option since 2011, according to the Missouri Independent 2024. A study done by the Missouri Department of Education found that no negative academic impact was shown in a four-day week if the instructional hours remained the same. Currently, Missouri law requires 1,044 hours in a school year. The four-day workweek was originally born due to rural districts not being able to hire and retain good teachers. Leeton School District in Central Missouri, recently decided to move to a four-day workweek for the 2024-2025 school year. Superintendent Adam Easterwood cited, "... teacher retention and recruitment as the motivating factors." Easterwood also mentioned, "... that this initiative would create a better home life and work life for students, faculty, and staff" (Nixon 2024).

Other districts that have adopted the four-day workweek require teachers to work at school two of the four days off each month. As with many things, each district could develop what works best for them. Currently, many districts utilize early release days or late start days for teacher collaboration. Adopting a four-day workweek would eliminate early release and late start days. I know that the current commissioner of education in Missouri, Margie Vandeven, worries that the four-day workweek is not giving struggling students enough time to learn. It will be interesting to hear what incoming commissioner Karla Eslinger has to say about this issue when she takes office in June 2024.

Another advantage a four-day workweek offers is the elimination of bus drivers, custodians, paraprofessionals, and cafeteria workers on the fifth day, resulting in potential district savings. These employees may then seek other part-time jobs outside the district. Additionally, running a seven-period day instead of block scheduling at the middle and high school levels saves districts revenue. This doesn't require as many teachers as does block scheduling, and in my opinion, it is better for student retention because they see each teacher every day.

Some districts have started offering childcare as an incentive to keep teachers in their districts. Other larger districts have developed affordable housing specifically for teachers. Perhaps schools could offer free lunches for employees and their children who attend school.

Teacher shortage gaps have been filled in many districts by adopting the Growing Your Own Teachers program, an alternative pathway to becoming an educator. According to researchers, as of the spring of 2022, an estimated 900 United States districts were using these programs to ease their teacher shortages. Grow Your Own Teacher apprenticeship programs now have access to millions of dollars in federal job-training funds through new United States Labor Department guidance. One program to grow teachers may target school employees, while another may focus on military veterans, college students, or even K-12 students, with some starting as young as middle school (NPR). Roddy Theobald, deputy director of the Center for Analysis of Longitudinal Data and Research says, " A challenge is that Grow Your Own programs rarely target the specific needs of schools Perhaps your district or state has a shortage in special education or STEM fields, and local programs may not have graduating teachers in those areas, leading to too many teachers in some areas and not enough in needed areas." Because this is a new program, not much data yet exists to evaluate the program's effectiveness .

Other ideas for improving schools could include year-round school. This would be beneficial for student retention. Because of the summer slide, much of this regression would be eliminated. It would also help the children of families who constantly struggle to keep food on the table, to receive two nutritious meals per day. Of course, there would be the same number of days off, just not altogether like we currently have in June, July and August.

Another potential savings would be only bussing students living a mile or farther from school. Perhaps this would only require one route of buses instead of two or more. Also, if teachers are teaching **all** students,as they should, there should be no need for gifted teachers.

For many years studies have revealed teenagers need more sleep and they should not start school until later; yet many schools continue starting middle school and high schools earlier than elementary schools. According to Kyla Washington, a senior research fellow at the University of Minnesota in the College of Education and Human Development, " A biological shift occurs in teenager's brains that causes them not to feel sleepy until about 10:45 or 11 at night". State Representative John Ray Clemmons from Nashville tried to pass a bill mandating later start times in 2022. He said, "Waking a teen at 7 a.m. is like waking one of us at 4 a.m. (Sweeney 2023)." Sleep deprivation leads to depression, health issues, lack of motivation especially for school, mental health issues, worse grades, and traffic accidents.

I do realize that if times were adjusted for middle and high school students, parents might have to secure childcare after school until older siblings arrive home to watch their younger siblings; but many parents can work from home now post-COVID and as parents we make adjustments all the time. Resistance to later start times is less about science than it is about logistical and financial difficulties, especially with basics like busing. If we want what is best for students, what is best for test scores, and what is best for our country, why would we not want to make this change? I can see no reason why, other than convenience.

I discussed the topic of recruiting "volunteer teachers" earlier in the chapter. They could man a second shift for students to stay after school, thus offering reteaching, accelerated teaching, or fun electives. Test scores would surely go up. This could also help parents with after-school care. Increasing the school day by two hours would again help accommodate the after school care for younger children and have great results in raising students to grade level standards. Again, there would have to be logistics worked out for students at middle school and high school athletics and other after-school activities, unless as discussed earlier we leave those to clubs or have morning practices.

In 1982, Jaime Escalante of Los Angeles, California, had great success as a math teacher raising **all** test scores in his classes. He would do whatever it took to raise scores. For instance, if a student missed two days of his class, he would call that student's parents and say just about anything he could dream up to motivate the parents to get their child to school. He attributed his success to four factors: having high expectations for all students, creating more time for learning, using standardized tests as benchmarks of progress, and creating team spirit (Mathews 2010 as cited by Weber 2010). Teachers often reminded students their school was a team and a family. They pledged to help one another in every way. The faculty let their students know that their school was a safe place (Matthews 2010 as cited by Weber 2010).The students enrolled in my career lab class have heard me say more than once what happens with us stays with us because we are a family.

As I mentioned earlier, it seems that more fights and gun violence are occurring in schools. It appears everyone is just angry! I believe each school building should have a therapy dog. I have seen three of these dogs at work at both the elementary and high school levels. As grumpy students arrive on the bus in the morning and see the dog, with tail wagging, their whole demeanor changes. This should be a change that requires no thought, just do it!

I also believe school uniforms could reduce many disciplinary infractions which occur at schools. School uniforms can break down class barriers because all students dress alike; it is more difficult to distinguish between students in higher social classes from those in lower classes. There is some evidence to indicate students have fewer distractions if they are dressed alike. This would also allow teachers and administrators to focus on their jobs instead of, for instance,checking t-shirts for inappropriate sayings and worrying about excessive skin exposure. Uniforms also promote a sense of community and tradition. Additionally, school uniforms can help create a safer environment as anyone not in uniform would be identified as a stranger in a building. (Josephson 2). Some might argue uniforms would take away individualism, but students can dress any way they prefer outside of school. Many jobs require uniforms so this would be a good introduction. Uniforms may be more expensive than typical school clothes; but I'm convinced schools could receive donations from businesses to offset that cost.

Every high school must guarantee the safety of its students, teachers, staff, and visitors and all schools should be free of drugs, weapons, and gangs. School leaders should build a climate of trust and respect to encourage peaceful solutions to conflict, and respond directly to any bullying, verbal abuse, or other threats (The Alliance for Excellent Education as cited by Weber 2010,219). There must be zero tolerance for these types of behaviors, and enforcement of consequences is essential. School districts and administrators are in a tough position to try to project the next tragedy. What are districts to do with LBGTQ+ students, like Nex Benedict, to keep them safe while being free to express who they are without infringing on other students' rights? This problem will not go away without some lines drawn in the sand and people being vocal about what is right.

March 8, 2024, in Jefferson City, Missouri, state representative Republican Jamie Gragg is trying to pass House Bill 2885. This proposed bill would make teachers, who support transgender students or those socially transitioning, register as sex offenders. If we recognize that we have a teacher shortage now, this will certainly cause many teachers to leave the profession and not for the reason you might think. Most teachers would not be afraid of the “sex offender” label or even going to jail for what they believe in, but teachers would never agree not to love and support their students unconditionally. “While this egregious bill is expected to die in committee hearings, it is increasingly alarming to watch extremist state legislators peddle anti-trans hate and continue to introduce discriminatory policies,” Willingham-Jaggers, executive director of GLSEN said in a statement to CNN. “Hate speech, especially when enshrined into discriminatory policies like these transphobic bills in Oklahoma and Missouri, leads to hate crimes” (Duster) and death, such as Nex. When and why did politics enter schools? There should be no place in schools for politics; our legislators should be addressing so many important issues. **Leave education to the educators!**

Every school should provide all students and teachers with the books, computers, laboratory equipment, technology, and other resources they need to be successful. All schools should maintain safe, clean facilities that are fit for teaching and learning (The

Alliance for Excellent Education as cited by Weber 2010). A clean and well-maintained school gives students a chance to be proud of their school and take ownership.

All community members should have easy access to information that gives clear, straightforward pictures of how well the school is serving all its students. Some of the key pieces of information include a school's graduation requirements, graduation and dropout rates, and student performance on state tests. The school is an indicator for the community, reflecting the good or bad trends that are changing the neighborhood. "Success breeds success and failure breeds failure" (Strickland 1971 as cited by Weber 2010).Students are successful and excel when all adults involved with them, parents, teachers,administrators, and community members, work together as a team to focus on the student as a whole, including student achievement and social development (Weingarten 2010 as cited by Weber 2010).

How will United States schools be successful again? I believe looking at the way European schools operate is worth exploring. In Europe, students start high school in the seventh grade and end in the twelfth grade. These schools rarely offer options for electives, and if they do, it will mostly be only one class. Students usually have ten classes throughout the year, but they only have six to eight classes each day. Depending on the importance of the class, students may take all five classes for five days, three days, two days, or in some cases only one day a week, similar to how some universities operate. Teachers are the ones rotating to students who stay in one room; this greatly reduces potential discipline problems during class change and limits the spread of viruses throughout the building.

European schools do not have clubs, sports, plays, or any other type of extracurricular activities. If students want to be involved in these activities, they will have to do it after school in centers that offer them at a cost or free.

An exchange student, Aru Armangeldi from Kazakhstan, currently attending Southern Garrett High School in America said, “I feel like if you want to study, Europe gives you much more opportunity to study, but if you just want to chill, not worry about your grades, hang out with friends, and go to after-school practices, then definitely American school is better” (Grajera 2023). Is this the reputation we want for American Schools?

Students in Europe usually do all their work by hand as compared to the U.S. using technology. Students take notes by hand and do all their homework in notebooks. Tests are also done on paper. Some believe the act and motion of physically writing helps with retention. School funding tends to be equal for European schools. This is not necessarily the case in the United States.

While here in the United States, students take tests like the SATs, ACTs, and AP exams, other countries have their versions. In European countries students are tracked in schools, based on individual academics and achievements.

We need not even go to Europe because here in the United States in New York we have examples of different types of high schools that are working. Students in New York City high schools must fill out an application before entering the ninth-grade year. There are nine specialized high schools in New York for top-performing students. Eight of these schools rely on a single-test admissions policy, depending on how students in the eighth or ninth grade perform on the specialized high school admissions test. This test is only offered one weekend in the fall (www.schools.nyc.gov). The nine specialized schools are:

- Bronx High School of Science
- The Brooklyn Latin School
- Brooklyn Technical High School
- High School for Mathematics, Science, and Engineering at City College
- High School for American Studies at Lehman College

- Queens High School for the Sciences at York College
- Staten Island Technical High School
- Stuyvesant High School
- Fiorello H. LaGuardia High School of Music & Art and Performing Arts

I understand that most districts could not afford to operate this many schools. In fact, the majority of districts serve far less students than the New York District serves, but with some creativity, schools could have more options for their students. For instance, we have a university close by, where we send students from the high school to certain core classes for dual credit. Could we expand this to band, music, art, and performing arts? We teach foreign languages at high school but not at middle school. Could we arrange for students to go to the high school to take foreign language classes? I currently take three middle schoolers to the high school for geometry. Students can attend our career center beginning their junior year of high school that offers classes in auto body and auto technology, cosmetology, health occupations, computer programming, and computer repair; but why can't these be offered early in the high school years? Could we partner with universities or local businesses to have students job shadow or learn hands-on skills? We must think outside of the box to develop more opportunities for students earlier in their academics to meet their needs so we don't lose them, especially for those who do not want to attend college. Our local hospital has opportunities for job shadowing or the opportunity to work alongside hospital personnel in all areas. We must take advantage of these opportunities available to our students. What are we waiting for?

Why would we not track students in the United States? If students are more academically alike in classes, they would be more eager to participate because they wouldn't be intimidated by the perceived smarter students. Each group of students could get more of what they need. This is how I was taught as an elementary student. I believe this is what some people are talking about when they say we should return to the basics. Teachers would love it if students were tracked because it would allow them to see legitimate growth among all their students. If a student was able to "catch up" to those in the next higher group, they could be moved. I believe tracking could benefit students through their freshman year of high school. After that, students could be put in classes together, better emulating the real world.

Another solution to improve schools is allowing more time for regular education teachers and special education teachers to collaborate about shared students. Most regular education teachers are handed a piece of paper or given a link to a student's IEP. They are supposed to read it along with maybe 20 other IEPs and remember the modifications and accommodations for each student. Then, on their own time they are to provide feedback to the case manager about the progress of each IEP student. Most colleges only require one class on IEPs, so many regular education teachers feel in the dark without time to properly talk to the special education teachers about each student on their roster.

Why in the United States do we hold our high school students hostage? Students who don't necessarily want to be at school often cause trouble in classes or around the building and fail classes anyway. Not all students are book- smart, but that certainly doesn't mean that there is not a place for them in society where they can be successful and happy. I believe that after a student's freshman year of high school, they should be given an exit exam much like the ones used in European schools. University-bound students in Europe take comprehensive end exams after grades twelve or thirteen. Those students who don't plan to attend a university can leave school after the tenth grade.

In the United States, if students can pass this exam, there is no need for them to stay at the high school if they do not want to be there. This would allow those not applying themselves at school to test out and pursue whatever they choose. Some of these students could be the ones causing trouble and feeling trapped, and now they have the option to leave. They would be free to go to trade schools or pursue other interests. School is painful for some students. Those who pass these high-stakes tests would have a choice to stay and receive enrichment or accelerated programs to further prepare them for college or move on. Those who do not pass the test could be placed in specific remedial classes geared toward their weaknesses to assist them to mastery. Because we would be losing some students in this process due to testing out, class sizes would be smaller, and a more specific curriculum tailored to individual needs could be utilized.

Often schools put their best teachers with academically advanced students, but this is not the best practice. A school's best teachers should be working with the academically lower students or lowest levels of education.

When developing the master schedule for the next school year, schedule IEP students first. Place them in the classes they need for graduation and then build everyone else's schedule around that. If teachers must vary their customary schedule,that is okay. Change keeps us all fresh and on top of our game, and education is a student-centered occupation. We are here to do what is best for kids. Base your co-teaching classes on where the IEP students fall in the schedule, keeping in mind that no more than one-third of the class should be identified as special services.

As the eighth grade IEP students I currently work with preparing to transition to high school, the process coordinators and current teachers sit down and discuss which high school classes the IEP students should take. This conversation takes place in early March. I recommended that one of my students have co-teaching or para support in both civics and physical science. The high school process coordinator that they don't have those available. I said, "You are going to have to offer these because that is what the student needs." I have a hard time understanding this logic because creating the master schedule has not even begun yet. Students' needs should be the priority. If we are trying to level the playing field for all students, this is the way it must be done.

When is too long for teachers and administrators to remain one position? Do they become complacent? I believe that anyone who does the same thing repeatedly, settles in and stops dreaming and wanting to make things better. The teacher is comfortable, easily becoming lazy or complacent. My suggestion would be for no one to stay in the same position for more than ten years without changing grade levels, subject matter, subject level, or buildings. This keeps us fresh, and we learn new things with new challenges.

As far as student discipline goes, that should be the easiest part of an administrator's job. Each district should have a discipline handbook for all identified infractions. Once the student receives a discipline referral, all that must be done is to look in the handbook and it spells out in black and white what the consequence should be, simple enough. This removes all subjectivity and does not make it personal. The difficult part is when the parents don't agree with the consequences. It should not matter. The discipline handbook is a board-approved document, and parents don't need to agree with the consequences. The parents can read the handbook with the infractions and consequences listed for each. The problem occurs when administrators are intimidated by parents and don't follow protocol. This practice hurts the administrator's credibility with students, teachers, and parents. If your handbook states after eight tardies students will receive consequences, follow through or don't have it in your discipline handbook. If your handbook states students are only allowed five minutes for restroom passes, you better call the students down that violate this. Just as we ask teachers to follow established building and classroom rules, so must administration. Not following through on handbook rules and regulations creates frustration for the teachers who are following protocol, and they lose faith in you.

Departments of Education should be responsible for providing the necessary resources for a school to succeed. Are there enough teachers for the school to maintain appropriate class size? Are there sufficient custodial services for the school? Is there an adequate supply of textbooks and/or laptops/iPads? Is the school equipped with science labs? A library? Is the State Department of Education making sure the school provides meaningful, effective professional development for staff (Weingarten 158)? The Federal Department of Education and State Department of Education should provide money and resources but should not be involved directly in the education process and mandates. I love that the United States supports other countries in their time of need; this is one of our unique characteristics that makes us America. I do believe however that we should take care of ourselves. More money should be allocated for teacher salaries so we can maintain the best. After all, education affects everyone! As far as what should be taught and how, this should be left up to the professionals, the teachers in the trenches and the ones who know their students. I truly feel that politics has no place in education. Of course, these departments of education should monitor each state's educational programs to make sure all policies and procedures are being followed. When there is accountability for everyone, everyone is accountable to each other, and most importantly, everyone is accountable to the students, top to bottom and bottom to top.

I have always believed and still believe that education is the greatest profession in the world. It is now or never, no more time to waste to save the state of education. We must decide what kind of educational system we are going to have. There is a lot of work to be done, important decisions to be made, and mindsets changed, but by working together as a community, parents, and school, we can bring the United States back as a front-runner in the world in all categories.

We cannot afford not to examine every solution presented as a possible solution to our educational woes. Do not try to reinvent the wheel and look to other districts for success. However, this process cannot take forever. The school superintendent must move quickly and thoroughly involving stakeholders. They must be confident, precise, and comfortable with their decisions on how to revamp their school district to the best it can be, and stay with this for at least four years to determine its success.

So, let's begin with renewed energy and hope, with faith and discipline, everyone together, until our work is done and we have the educational system and world we can all be proud of once again.

Summary

No one is questioning being an administrator is difficult, and, depending on the size of the district you can wear many hats. There is no time to waste in turning around the American Educational system. Not only are there not enough teachers, but some of the current teachers aren't good for our students or good for education. We must start by releasing ineffective teachers and replacing them with good teachers.

I am certain that if teacher pay increases, we will have more people returning to education. Many who traded their passion for pay would now be able to fulfill their dream. A program being used to develop teachers is the " Grow Your Own Program." Teacher certification requirements are also being examined for possible revisions.

Districts need to ask for help from businesses and community members who have employees with expertise in areas that could complement the current school system. We need to expand the definition of "teacher." Many retirees could offer valuable experiences. Appreciate everyone in your building :custodians, nurses, cooks, social workers, secretaries, and counselors. We all must work together.

If we want to be a world leader in education, we need to focus on content and rigor like European countries. They don't offer extra-curricular activities that take students' focus away from studies. European schools also allow students who are not college-bound to leave school after the tenth grade. One possible solution is to adopt one of New York's secondary school options for those not necessarily planning to attend college.

Why do we ignore the fact that for years we have known that teenagers need to start school later in the day to be successful? We continue to leave start times as they are because it would be difficult for parents to find childcare. If we want what is best for our students, we need to rearrange the start time for our elementary and secondary students.

School uniforms would help with class designation and could potentially help with discipline referrals and safety.

Therapy dogs could help with discipline and act as stress reducers.

Four-day workweeks and year-round school would benefit both students and teachers alike.

Departments of Education need to provide money and all the resources to make schools successful, but as far as educational mandates they need to leave that to the experts, the people in the trenches. As a nation more money needs to be allocated to teacher salaries so we can keep the best of the best.

Superintendents have no time to waste in deciding which direction their district needs to go to improve student performance. Once a decision has been made, with your director of curriculum on board, proper training and materials need to be available to all involved. The implementation of this initiative needs to be consistent and unwavering without change for a designated period.

Conclusion

The United States Educational System is in trouble. Collectively we can do better. We all have the same end goal: educating our students to again become a world leader in education. Communication between parents and school must extend both ways. Superintendents need to communicate with each building, and building administrators need to be transparent with their staff.

Many things need to be changed and skills honed to attain this. Parents need to be present and be involved with their students. Parents need to be supportive of the school and the teachers. If parents cannot help students with their assignments, they need to seek help for them. Many schools have tutoring, churches offer tutoring, and private agencies are available in most cities.

Parents must monitor their children's activities and friends to watch for signs of depression, drug and alcohol use, bullying, and mental illness. Parents also should monitor the social media accounts of their children. Students look for role models and in the absence of one at home, they will look elsewhere. All adults need to strive to be positive role models.

Peaceful protests have always been the way change has occurred in our country. However, somewhere it became displaced by people wanting to inflict pain on someone for just disagreeing with them. This is wrong. Kindness, compassion, and understanding are the best character traits to strive for. It is okay to disagree with someone and move forward without violence. If this is modeled by parents, teachers, and all adults nationwide, we can change and save our world. If students want a hug from a teacher or administrator, hug them. They need that connection and a feeling of closeness. Those are the relationships and connections we seek.

Schools need to do a better job of identifying and disciplining bullies. There is no place in public education for bullies, including teachers. Students should feel safe to be who they are without worrying about their safety, whether it be mental, emotional, or physical. Our loyalty should be to the person being bullied, not the bullying.

Public schools accept everyone, but there are other choices for parents in deciding where their students should go to school. Private schools and charter schools, although they have some stipulations attached, are alternatives to public school education. Charter schools and private schools remove the possibility of equity for all students. Some parents choose to homeschool their children.

COVID-19 not only set students back academically but caused much more mental stress and anxiety, creating more mental illness. Parents and schools alike need to monitor students closely to watch for signs of this. Again, there are many agencies available to help struggling students. The school has counselors on staff and there are outside agencies in many cities to help with these issues. I also included a phone number and internet link, stress scales, and relaxation techniques that may be helpful.

Let's increase the physical education requirement to help with obesity. Classes that include movement and community service activities could meet this criterion.

IEPs specific to each student should be followed. If assignments/tests are to be modified, then **true modifications** should be made. If accommodations are supposed to be made, **they must be made.** Accommodations and modifications are not interchangeable terms. Special education teachers are more than willing to assist with these modifications or accommodations.

Most teachers are great people, hard workers, and good teachers. Teaching is like any other profession that has mostly good but some bad. Teachers must communicate with students and parents. Teachers should know how each student learns best. This way teachers can create lessons geared toward student's strengths allowing them to receive a truer picture of what the student knows. I believe that if students were tracked it would be beneficial to be with other students like them and feel safe to speak and ask questions. Tracking would allow teachers to tailor lessons to each group's ability level. This is how education was when I was in school. At some level we already do this in math classes, particularly in high schools and middle schools. We just need to be cognizant of how we label classes because we don't want to damage a student's self-esteem.

Every student should be required to take debate so they can learn how to listen and respond appropriately to others' points of view. Perhaps if we make this a priority at school, it will trickle down into the greater society and our country can start to heal. We have concertgoers throwing bottles and other items onto the stage at the performers.

Teachers must be consistent with their discipline and have high expectations that students will follow their rules.

Requiring school uniforms could reduce discipline problems and make schools safer. Teachers should be paid like the professionals they are. If teachers were paid representative of their worth for this highly responsible job, there would no longer be a teacher shortage. Federal and state governments must rise to the challenge if they want to save the United States Educational system.

Teachers need to be confident in their abilities and not tolerate fellow teachers who are not pulling their weight. If we all want what is best for students, we must approach those who are not doing their job. The term and concept of a “professional learning community” embodies this.

Administrators should reward those teachers who are doing their job well, but be prepared to replace ineffective ones. If principals have little or no control over who teaches in their school, they will likely inherit teachers who are bad fits. There should be little or no external control, especially over personnel. Administrators should have the autonomy to hire and fire personnel to arm their school with the most qualified staff who believe in their administrator's vision.

Adding time to the day would help justify the increased salary for teachers and help those struggling students learn skills in which they are weak. This could also help parents with after-school care. Most teachers stay well past the required time anyway.

We must make connections with students, so they feel safe and comfortable with at least one adult in every building they are in. This will allow students to share things with us that could save lives.

Students will tell us what they need if we just allow them to. They have great ideas, and they are our future.

As a Nation, we need to reach out to those in our communities to ask for volunteer teachers.

Year-round school with four-day workweeks would help with both student and teacher retention.

Middle and high schools should be starting later than elementary schools; current schedules should be flip-flopped. If as a country we want to be world leaders again, our students need to focus on academics, not extracurriculars. We need not worry about after-school activities because there will be none.

All children can learn, and all neighborhoods can have great schools. We are only lacking a country of moms and dads armed with the truth and the conviction to change it (Guggenheim 2008 as cited by Weber 2010). The late President John Kennedy, in his inaugural address, on January 20, 1961, stated, "Ask not what your country can do for you, ask what you can do for your country." Now is the time to step it up for the good of our nation to restore our great educational system. Parents and citizens need to make noise about the state of education, demand more, and be willing to do their part. Partner with schools and teachers to help anyway you can. Demand that teachers receive more pay. Reach out to your representatives and let them know it is time to make education a priority.

It is not impossible to turn things around, but we are in the final hour. Our young people today are not afforded the opportunity to develop in the essential areas needed to move our country forward. Our students can not read or write cursive or count back change. Currently, most students in the United States can't read a clock unless it is digital. Many students have no idea where states are located within the United States because they rely on GPS. Students are missing out on other life skills as well. Some students lack manners and social skills required to make them productive citizens. Real changes need to be made and just placing a band-aid on the problem is not the answer this time. Each school district must get busy at the direction of the superintendent, involving current students and teachers within the district, and collectively decide what they believe is the best for students. Ultimately, the final decision rests in the hands of the superintendent who must move swiftly because there is no time to waste.

I love the education process. I love teaching, teachers, and students. I wholeheartedly believe that it is teachers, not professional athletes, musicians, or politicians, who perform the most important job in the world; without educators, none of us would be where we are today. We can all do better. We must do better. The late Stephen Hawking said, "If you look behind every exceptional person, there is an exceptional teacher."

Things I Have Experienced or Heard Over the Years' Worth Sharing

I had a student that had CP and was in a wheelchair. A physical therapist only came once a week, so the rest of the time it was up to her parents and I to get her out of her chair and stretch her. I think I was much more consistent at therapy than her parents were. She never missed school. She also got very messy at lunch so we would often have to take her into the restroom to clean her up after lunch. She had missed several days of school and I was worried about her, wondering what was going on. On her first day back at school we were in the restroom cleaning up after lunch and she said, "Boy am I going to be sore tomorrow." I said, "Why is that?" She replied, "You know, the **F WORD !"** My mind was going everywhere, and I did not want to ask the question, but knew I had to. "What F word?" She said," You know, **ferapy!"** Therapy, what a relief! Loved this girl!

There was about to be a school dance and two students from my self-contained class were going to attend. The boy asked the girl to the dance by saying, "Will you go to the dance with me? I can't do any better and you can't do any worse."

Ms. Reynolds, I won't be able to spell very good today because I fell off the slide and hurt my wrist.

I got some new tennis shoes and I'm going to be able to run so fast.

I was working in my yard one spring weekend day when one of my eighth-grade students walked by and asked if this was where I lived. He introduced a friend he was with. As he left, I found myself thinking that I wasn't sure I was happy about him knowing where I lived. Later that afternoon my doorbell rang, and it was the same student. He said, "I didn't know where else to go, I accidentally ejaculated in my girlfriend, and I need a pregnancy test." In thirty years, I had never been asked this question or anything like it. I told him how long it would take to show up positive or negative on the test and that it would take me about an hour to get the test, but I would get it for him. I went and bought the test, and explained to him how the test worked and how long it would take for it to show up if she was pregnant. I also reminded him that he and I had previously talked about him having sex. He said that he remembered and thanked me. That student never stopped by my house again. He is the student who affectionately refers to me as grandma.

One of my students, who happened to have Down syndrome, wanted me to play golf with him. His father worked at the golf course, and he had spent a lot of time there. I agreed that I would. When I arrived at the course that day his father had a golf cart already for us to go. It was a three-wheel cart. He wanted to drive so I let him. He had the pedal to the medal and was giggling as we bounced around. He went to turn going too fast and the cart started to tip. Because I was heavier, I jumped out of the cart so it would level out. It was silent for what seemed like an hour. When he finally spoke, he said, "Heart Attack!" I said, "If you promise me that you will never drive that fast again, I will not tell your parents." He said, "All right."

A couple of years after this the same student was missing from high school. The police station called the school to inform them that this student was at their office. He had turned himself in because he had tried a cigarette, and he was not old enough to smoke.

I can't sit down because I have ants in my pants, and they are making me dance.

Each day as students in my self-contained classroom left my room, they attended a special, art, music, or P.E. One specific student would ask me each day as he left if he had to go to class or if he could go home. Of course, I would always answer, "Yes, you have to go to class." One day, He asked the question, and my response was,' I don't care where you go when you leave here." A little bit later my principal arrived at my room, and he asked if I had told this young man he could leave. I shared with him exactly what I had said to the student. My principal started laughing, he said that he had seen the boy go out the door and called his name and the student kept running as fast as he could away from the school.

While in my replaced science class at the high school I had allowed students to work together on a project. A group of 2 boys were working together and one of them kept tapping his finger on the desk. The other boy had told him to stop because it was driving him crazy. When it was time to go back to their desks for the next part of the lesson, they begged me to stay together promising that they would pay attention and be good. I allowed them to stay together. I was reading from the textbook and the students were to follow along. I started reading and I heard the tapping start on the desk again As I continued to read, I looked up over the top of the book and said, "If you don't stop that I'm going to cut your pecker off!" I quickly looked back down at the pages of the book, waited a minute, and then looked back over the top of the book at the students. They were all staring at me and when our eyes met, we all started laughing for about 2 minutes. That moment was never spoken about again until 4 years later when one of the boys was getting ready to graduate. He asked me, "Do you still remember what you said?" He said, "That was funny." I had to agree with him. This boy is now a man and one of the custodians at the high school we work in and is wonderful at what he does.

Recently in the girls' restroom at the high school, I heard myself saying, "There is only supposed to be one person in the stall at a time, and if you're not going,get out so those that have to go can!"

We were discussing first impressions and how important it is to be clean from head to toe, with fingernails cut and clean, a good haircut and clean hair, and clean clothes. I commented that it isn't necessarily fair because the way we look on the outside doesn't define who we are, and that people meeting us for the first time can't see our hearts and know who we are. Then one of my students raised his hand and said, "Why can't everyone have an x-ray so we can see everyone's heart." If it were only this simple.

The other assistant principal and I loved to tease each other. She always referred to me as the nice one. She was absent from school for a few weeks because of medical issues. We would email back and forth occasionally so she could stay up on what was going on at school. We were experiencing some growing pains, and a few teachers were going to have to relocate to another room in the school. (This is not uncommon; I think I moved 5 times in 9 years). One teacher, probably one of the nicest people I've ever met, had to move rooms and wasn't happy about it. I shared this with the other assistant principal. I jokingly told the other assistant principal that I had told the teacher, "To f-ing suck it up and not to act like a baby!" I waited but I got no response back from her. I waited a couple of days and called her and asked why she hadn't said anything about what I had told the teacher? She said, "I don't know what you are talking about." I thought she was joking but she assured me that she wasn't. I quickly looked back through my emails. I don't know how it happened, but I had sent the terrible email to the teacher and not the other assistant principal. I felt terrible, as I should have. I immediately called my friend who was the district PR person and told her I had a PR nightmare and explained the situation. She told me that I needed to go to the teacher and explain what had happened. I went to the teacher's room and explained what had happened and told her how sorry I was. I was so ashamed of myself. She started crying and said she thought that she had done something! I would not have ever done this in any other circumstance.

Always, Always, Always, check to see who you are sending an email to.

In my self-contained EMH classroom, we were discussing the effects of different substances on the body. Smoking was brought up and pregnant women should not smoke. One of my students raised his hand and said, “My momma smoked when she was pregnant with me and there’s nothing wrong with me.” What great self-esteem he had.

When I was principal at the elementary school, I had a teacher who was pregnant and was struggling to come up with a name for the baby. I had just watched Saturday Night Live where they were talking about naming a baby f-ing because it would go with everything. Johnny f-ing Smith, Chloe f-ing Johnson etc. During her plan period, I got on the intercom that only went to her room and told her that she could name the baby f-ing. I told her the story without taking a breath and then waited for her response. I was really surprised when she said, “I have parents here.” I said,” No you don’t!” Then I hear a male voice. I waited until the parents came downstairs and I stopped them and explained. Luckily, they had a great sense of humor and were very understanding.

Before I became an administrator, I taught summer school P.E. for those students who had not gotten their credit or had failed it previously. We were on the track and the sprinklers turned on the football field. The students asked if they could run through them. I said that they could. When class was over, the students left for the day someone shared with me that sewer water was watering the field. I had all these scenarios running through my mind. I was worried that the students were going to get sick, and I'd have to call the parents and let them know. I mentioned it to someone, and they let me know that it was watered by a well and not the sewer. I felt so much better.

While teaching high school, we were doing a lesson on our senses. I put together some random household items in a sack. Students were chosen to be blindfolded and reach into the bag and identify the object just by touch. If they couldn't identify them, we would pull it out and I would explain what it was. One of the objects that stumped them was a meat tenderizer. Apparently, at that moment, I could not think of the word tenderizer. So, I said, "You know it is what you beat your meat with, a meat beater." No explanation is needed!

While doing the summer school principal internship at the kindergarten building each day at dismissal, we would put each student in their parent's car for safety reasons. One day I got a little girl who was a limited English speaker and tried to put her into a car that wasn't her parents. I will never forget the look on the man's face as I tried to put someone else's child into his car. I'm sure you all know the emoji with the big bulging eyes, that was his expression!

I had to sit in with the assistant principal as he was meeting with a parent whose daughter was on my caseload. It was a disciplinary meeting because the girl had taken off her clothes and was going to be suspended for a while. The assistant principal told the parent the girl was going to be out of school for a certain period of time for disrobing in class. The parent said, “Well what did she do?” The assistant principal said, “She took off her clothes.” The parent finally understood what her daughter had done. Sometimes we need to remember to use the “ kiss principle" (keep it simple stupid).

The same young lady had to be suspended for a while. During lunch at an alternative school she and a boy were caught having oral sex. The girl did not understand why she was in trouble because it was during her lunch shift and not academic time.

My son, his girlfriend, and I had gone out to dinner. Neither one of them finished their food and we were getting to-go boxes. I said to my son, “why don’t you put your meat in her box!”When it came out of my mouth I couldn’t believe how it sounded.

We were facing items on the shelf at Walgreens during the career lab class. When we got to the laxatives my student said, “I used to think if you took enough of these it would take away all the fat!" I told him, "I understand how you could have thought that."

Four utility poles went down and all electricity at the middle school was knocked out and students were released early. The electric company was not sure they would have power restored for school the next day. Remarkedly all power was restored, and the school was up and running the next day. A student asked if the power was on. The teacher responded, "What do you think?" The student then says, "I don't know that's why I asked you."

When I was teaching health/science at the high school I had a class of ten, four girls and six boys. We were discussing reproduction. I decided to bring in bananas and condoms to teach the students' safe sex. I thought the lesson went well until the spring when three of my four girls became pregnant. I never taught this lesson again.

During black history month, students were to research a black person in history and create a poster talking about the person they chose. The students had to share with the teacher and be approved before they began their project.One young man wanted to do Abraham Lincoln.

While teaching a basketball unit to a high school gym class one of my friends told the students to put their balls on the floor. All the male students in class sit down on the gym floor.

We were reviewing our states and when I asked where Virginia was located, one of my boys started laughing. I knew he thought I had said vagina.

My freshman year of high school was the first year for girls' basketball. We had our first game, and everyone was expected to take a shower before heading home. I am very modest and was more worried about this than anything else. I quickly took a shower, wrapped my towel around me, and proceeded to jog to the locker room to get dressed. Like all gym locker rooms, the floor was concrete, and I slipped and fell, spread eagle in front of everyone. I never showered at school again. I waited until I got home.

As we were returning to the building from working in the community the temperature had dropped about ten degrees from when we left, and the wind had picked up. I was telling my career lab students that I was cold. One of my students said, "That is because you are elderly, and elderly people get cold more easily."

Acknowledgements

I believe that everything that happens in our life is supposed to happen and all the people that cross our paths are meant to have an impact on us in some way. Even though some relationships turn out poorly, if you look deeply enough you will find the lesson in each interaction. I know I have learned so much from adults and students. If you just listen to others you meet we all have a message. These people help shape our lives and thoughts.

To all those who have inspired me over the years and there is no way I can list them all, just know I thank you and you matter.

First and foremost, the good Lord above who gives me strength every day and has brought wonderful people into my life.

My sons, Gabe and Ben. Even though they tease me about a lot of things, they have only been supportive of me in writing this book. I love you both very much, am so proud of you and am blessed to be your mom.

My Dad, I know that he is watching down from heaven and is proud of me. I carry him with me everywhere I go.

Woods Prael and Susan Crooks, it was our conversation that started me thinking and wondering what I could do to make a difference.

Vicky Reynolds Thomann, you were the first to read my first draft and have encouraged me along the way. I love you, cousin.

Penny Easterwood, you always encouraged me after I told you I was doing this. You are such an amazing person and friend. Thank you for your proofreading and editing, without you this would never have happened. You're the sister I never had. I love you.

Shelbie Dalton, you inspire me to continue working hard each day as you do, even when things aren't easy. Also, your continued support and encouragement. I love you.

Carol Hassler for reading and editing my draft. Your help has been so appreciated and valuable. Without you none of this would have happened. Your friendship over the years has meant even more. I love you.

Simone Dillingham, you taught me more about being a good administrator and friend than you could imagine. You have always supported me in anything I have done or who I am. I love you.

Discovery team thanks for letting this old lady be part of your team and being supportive of me writing this book. I made it.

Elois Pelton,Susan Seipp,Norma Dunn, Mr. and Mrs. Brown, Ginny and Phil Dorth, Gloria Brown, Judy Rittman, Dinks Elwell, Jane Markert, Peggy Martin, Milly Barnes, Jan Brandt, Ron Harmon, Dudley Schnakenberg, Scott Patrick, Doc VanDam, Bob Thompkins, Patty Dinges, Cathy McGrath,Joan Parks, Nancy Gilbertson, and Ronda Miles. All former teachers and coaches helped shape me as a person and coach and were great examples of human beings, thank you.

All the students and teachers I have worked with have had an impact on my life.

Emotional Stress Scale

Psychiatrist Thomas H. Holmes of the University of Washington School of Medicine has developed a scale to measure the relative stress induced by various changes in a person's life.The amount of stress is measured on a point scale of 200"life -change units." Studies by DrHolmes and his associates show you accumulate more than 300 units in a single year, your life has probably been disrupted enough to make you vulnerable to illness.

Event	**Scale of Impact**
Death of a spouse	100
Divorce	73
Marital separation	65

Jail term	63
Death of a close family member	63
Personal injury or illness	53
Marriage	50
Fired at work	47
Marital reconciliation	45
Retirement	45
Change in health of family member	44
Pregnancy	40
Sex difficulties	39
Gain of new family member	39
Business readjustment	39
Change in financial status	38

Death of a close friend	37
Change to a different line of work	36
Change in number of arguments with spouse	35
Mortgage over $10,000	31
Foreclosure of mortgage or loan	30
Change in responsibilities at work	29
Son or daughter leaving home	29
Trouble with In-laws	29
Outstanding personal achievement	28
Spouse begins or stops work	26
Begin or end school	26
Change in living conditions	25
Revision of personal habit	24

Trouble with boss	23
Change in work hours and conditions	20
Change in residence	20
Change in schools	20
Change in recreation	19
Change in church activities	19
Change in Social activities	18
Mortgage or loan less than $10,000	17
Change in sleeping habits	16
Change in number of family get-togethers	15
Vacation	13
Christmas	12
Minor violation of the law	11

I wish I could give credit to the people that created the information provided below this point but these are handouts that I have had since undergraduate school and the author's identity has been lost. I cannot say for certainty but perhaps, this is another part of Dr. Holmes scales.

Signs Of Stress In Young Children

Daydreams frequently

Doesn't respond to friendly caregiver overtures

Has frequent prolonger temper tantrums

Solemn face and rarely smiles or laughs

Acts sullen, defiant and says " I don't care" when adult explains how their misbehavior has hurt another

Punishes self through slapping, head banging, or calling themself bad names

Is overly sensitive to mild criticism

Reports proudly to an adult they hurt another child

Has a constant need to sleep although not sick

Is hyperactive or restless, wanders around the room, touches and disturbs toys, games and others property

Has dull, vacant expression, as if trying to ward off thinking about stressful trauma or tries to deny stressful feelings

is highly demanding of adults although usually fairly self-sufficient

Is preoccupied with frightening images of monsters or other violent threatening figures

For much younger students, displays disturbed bodily functions, constipation or diarrhea, soils self frequently even after potty training

Is clumsy on easy manual tasks due to muscular tensions

Has nightmares

Bullies or scapegoats and may get other children to join in

Frequently acts aggressively against others, even adults

Please keep in mind several disorders such as ADHD, depression and autism mimic these signs, so we must be careful without testing to place labels on people.

Stress Scale for Children

Life Event	Value
Death of a parent	100
Parent's new relationship(new sibling involved)	90
Divorce of parents	73
Parents' new relationship	70
Separation of parents	65
Parent's jail term	63

Death of close family member (grandparent)	63
Personal injury or illness	53
Parent's remarriage	50
Suspension or expulsion from school	47
Summer vacation	46
Parents reconciliation	45
Parent or sibling illness	44
Mother's pregnancy	40
Anxiety over sex	39
Birth of a new baby	39
New school, classroom or teacher	39
Money problems at home	38
Death or moving away of a close friend	37

Death of a valued pet	37
Change in school work	36
More quarrels with parents or parents quarreling more	35
Change in school responsibilities	29
Siblings going away to school	29
Family arguments with grandparents	29
Winning school or community awards	28
Mother going to work or stopping work	26
School beginning or ending	26
Family's standard of living changing	25
Change in personal habits (bedtime, homework)	24
Trouble with parents, lack of communication	23
Change in school hours, schedule of courses	23

Family moving	20
A new school-high school	20
New sports, hobbies, family recreation activities	20
Change in church activities	19
Change in social activities-new friends, loss of old friends, peer pressure, teasing	18
Change in sleeping habits	16
Change in family get togethers	15
Change in eating habits going on or off a diet	15
Vacation other than summer	13
Christmas	12
Breaking home, school or community rules	11

Stress Scale For College Students

Below are listed events which occur in the life of a college student. Place a check in the left-hand column for each of those events that have happened to you during the last 12 months.

Life Event	Point Value
____ Death of a close family member	100
____ Jail term	80
____ Final year or first year of college	68
_____ Pregnancy to you or caused by you	60

____	Severe personal illness or injury	58
_____	Marriage	50
_____	Any interpersonal problems	45
_____	Financial difficulties	40
_____	Death of a close friend	40
_____	Arguments with your roommate	40
_____	Major disagreement with your family	40
_____	Major changes in personal habits	30
_____	Change in living environment	30
_____	Beginning or ending of a job	30
_____	Problem with your boss or professor	25
_____	Outstanding personal achievement	25
_____	Failure in some course	25

_____	Final Exams	20
_____	Increased or decreased dating	20
_____	Change in working conditions	20
_____	Change in major	20
_____	Change in your sleep habits	18
_____	Several day vacation	15
_____	Change in eating habits	15
_____	Family reunion	15

After checking the items above, add up the point value for all of the terms checked.

How Teachers And Caregivers Can Help Children Cope With Stress

1. Recognize when a child is stressed by being alert to changes in behavior, such as bedwetting or poor concentration.
2. Model self-control and coping skills yourself. Be fair and sensitive to differences and problems. Children mimic adult behavior.

   As parents or teachers, find social support in your life so that you are energized for adaptive coping with problems that arise.

3. Enhance children's self-esteem, wherever and whenever possible through encouragement,focused attention, and warm personal regard.
4. Encourage each child to develop a special interest or skill that can serve as an innersource of pride and self-esteem.
5. Anticipate stressful events and be proactive to award unnecessary stress.
6. Acknowledge children's feelings and give them permission to feel scared, lonely, or angry. Give children words to their negative feelings as they will not become aggressive.
7. Help children distinguish reality from fantasy. Children sometimes believe that because they did or did not do something expected of them they will be punished. An example of this could be, dad didn't come home because you, the child, were a sloppy eater or threw a fit because you didn't get an ice cream cone.

8. Structure classroom activities to enhance cooperation rather than competition. Children flourish where they can grow and achieve at their own pace.
9. Adults can locate reading materials to help children identify with similar characters and how they are coping with their stress. This allows the student to know they are not alone.
10. Use art. Many young children cannot verbally express fears and anger about painful stressors in their lives.Paint, clay, and other materials allow a child to express upsets and act out private feelings.

If you are a teacher working with a child under stress involving parents or caregivers allows you to work together. You and the family can be mutually supportive and reduce stressors and enhance the security of the child.

Ways To Reduce Stress

1. Get up 15 minutes earlier.
2. Prepare for morning the night before.
3. Never wear ill-fitting clothes.
4. Set appointments ahead.
5. Don't rely on your memory.
6. Practice Preventive maintenance.
7. Make duplicates of all keys.

8. Rearrange work hours, if possible.
9. Say " no" more often.
10. Never shop for clothes with critical teenagers, skinny friends or those who look terrific in everything.
11. Take advantage of off hours for banking and shopping.
12. Rearrange mealtimes.
13. Feed the children separately.
14. Keep an emergency supply of necessities.
15. Walk everywhere you can.
16. Make copies of all important papers and keep originals in a safe place.
17. Anticipate your needs.
18. Don't put up with anything that doesn't work properly.

19. Make advance reservations.

20. Allow extra time.

21. Be prepared to wait.

22. Never arrange a meeting place with no phone.

23. Find the humor in it.

24. Keep a busy kit handy when you travel.

25. Relax your standards.

26. Get help with the jobs you hate.

27. Establish a serene place of your own.

28. Change your perspective.

29. Count your blessings.

30. Memorize your favorite poems.

31.Keep a supply of individually wrapped candies or gum handy.

32. Travel light.

33. Be prepared for rain.

34. Ask questions.

35. Unclutter your life.

36. Make contingency plans.

37. Avoid reliance on chemical aids.

38. Find enjoyable ways to exercise.

39. Talk to a loving friend or relative.

40. Have a message.

41. Listen to podcasts.

42. Listen to eBooks.

Relaxation Techniques

Understand that relaxation cannot be forced and that your ability to relax may vary from time to time, but over time "relaxation habit" can be developed. Stick with the same method for at least 2 weeks, so that it becomes easy and a routine for you. It takes 21 days for a habit to form. Use it regularly for 5 to 10 minutes or more a day.

- Check your tension throughout the day by simply becoming aware of each part of your body from head to toe. Relax any tense muscles. Take several deep breaths when you begin feeling tense.

- Practice relaxation sitting up or lying down. Get into a comfortable position in a quiet place with your eyes closed.
- Concentrate on your breathing or on a peaceful scene.
- Take a slow, deep breath and focus on one part of your body. Become aware of any tension in those muscles.
- As you breathe out, relax your muscles and allow the tension to drain out.
- Concentrate on your breathing taking about 6 to 9 breaths a minute. you can count to yourself if you need to. In, one, two. Out, one, two. Move on to a new body part. As you breathe in, become aware of the tension. As you breathe out, release the tension, letting the muscles go limp.
- Don't ignore the muscles in your face, feet and hands.
- To end the slow , rhythmic breathing, count silently and slowly to 3. At the count of 3 take a deep breath, open your eyes, and begin moving slowly.

Yoga is also a great way to reduce stress. Places to practice yoga can be found in most cities. There are also many online yoga apps that you can download and practice at your leisure in the confines of your home.

Meditation has become popular for relaxation and can virtually be done anywhere. A person can create their own meditation routine or acquire one of the many available online.

For the past two years I have gotten a massage each month. This has helped keep me out of the chiropractic and releases muscle tension.

Pray also is a great way to de-stress.

However you choose to control stress in your life it is of utmost importance. You can't take care of anyone else if you're not taking care of yourself.

References

Austrew, A. (2022). How to Prevent Your Kids From Losing What They Learned in School During Summer Vacation. Scholastic

American Academy of Child & Adolescent Psychiatry (2011).

Barrington, I. (2022) Barrington Irving, Pilot and Education. National l Geographic, SAVVAS Learning Company LLC.

Barrington, K. (2003). The 15 Biggest Failures of the American Public Education Systemwww.publicschoolreview.com

Beers, K. and Probst, B. (2012). Notice and Note Strategies for Close

Reading. Portsmouth: NH. Heinemann Publishing.

Brown, M.and Latham A. (April 2024). Tennessee House passes bill allowing armed teachers, sending measure to the governor. Nashville Tennessean

Burke, L. Ph.D., Director of the Center for Education Policy at the Conservation Heritage Foundation. Which Fought the Common Core

Canada, G. (1998). *Reaching up for Manhood: Transforming the Lives of Boys in America*. President and CEO of the Harlem Children's Zone.

Cardoza, K. (2023). This teacher shortage solution has gone viral. But does it Work?www.npr.org

Chilcott, L. (2010). Waiting for "Superman" the film, producer

Dewey, C. (2024). Children's nutrition program, revved in the pandemic, faces severe cuts. Rhode Island Current

Duster, C. (2024). Proposed Missouri bill would make teachers register as sex offenders if found supporting students who socially transition. CNN.com

Dillion, J.T. (1988). *Questioning and teaching: A manual of practice*. New York: Teachers College Press.

Evans,M. (2024). Bible must be taught in Oklahoma schools, the state superintendent says. The Oklahoman.

Finwick, B. (2024). 'It could have been me': At Oklahoma vigil for Nex Benedict, mourners call for action. www.advocate.com

Fields, Dr. H. III (2021). *How to Achieve Educational Equity.* Howard E. Fields III.

Gamble, J. (2024). Oklahoma LGBTQ suicide prevention line sees more than 230% increase in calls since Nex Benedict's death. CNN

Gates, B. and M. (2009). *Educating America's Young People for the Global Economy*

Grajera, J. (2023). American vs European Schools: Which is really the best? The Lance

Grant, A. (2023). *Hidden Potential: The Science of Achieving Greater Things.* United States: Random House

Guggenheim, D. (2010). Waiting for "Superman" the film, writer, and director. Los Angeles: Paramount Studios.

Gun Violence Archive.gunviolenceacchive.org (2023).

Hanshaw, A. (2023) Eslinger Announced as Missouri's next

commissioner of education.Missouri Independent in Warrensburg Star Journal

Hanushek, E.A. (2009). *"Teacher Deselection" in Creating a New Teaching Profession.* Washington, DC: Urban Institute Press

Haworth, J. (2024). Mom arrested after making drink for son to give to school bully that hospitalized him. ABC News.

Helsel, P., (2024). Family of teen who died by suicide after video of her assault was posted online sues school. NBC NEWS

Hood, J., (1993). The Failure of American Public Education. Foundation for Economic Education.

Hurley, B., (2024). Oklahoma banned trans students from bathrooms. Now a bullied student is dead after a fight.

https://independent.co

Icard, M. (2023). *Bullying at School: What can parents do to help victims and stop bullies.*http//www.cnn.com

Josephson, A. (2023). The Pros and Cons of School Uniforms. Smartasset.com

Kane, T. (2023). Faculty Director of Center of Education Policy Research at Harvard University as quoted by Juan Cisneros, Should the school year be extended to make up for learning loss? CBS NEWS NEXSTAR.

Kekatos, M. (2024). Many students have not regained COVID-era losses in reading, math report finds. Read in ABC News: https://apple.news

Kern, J. (1990). *Build the Fort Today. San Antonia, TX:* The Desktop

Publishing Service

Lawlis, Dr. F. (2013). *NOT MY CHILD A PROGRESSIVE AND PROACTIVE APPROACH for Healing Addicted Teenagers and Their Families.* HAY HOUSE, INC. New York.

Lerer, L. (2024) On the Ballot in Iowa: fear. Anxiety. Hopelessness. The New York Times.

Luhby, T. (2024). New Program will help feed millions of kids over the summer, but not all states are participating. CNN Politics.

Mac, K. (2022). Some Iowa Teens Can Do Yard Work For P.E. Credit

Mather, K. (2024). Schools have spent millions on Yondr phone pouches, designed to keep Students off their devices. Are they worth it? Yahoo! news.

Matthews, J. (2009). *Work Hard. Be Nice. How Two Inspired Teachers Created the Most Promising Schools in America.* Chapel Hill, NC: Algonquin.

Mayes-Osterman, C. (2024). Assistant principal charged with felony child abuse in6-year-old's shooting of teacher. USA TODAY.

McCallum, W. (2020). *After 10 years of Hopes and Setbacks, What Happened toThe Common Core*. A lead writer of math standards for Common Core.

McCann, T.M. (2014). *Transforming talk into text: Argument writing, inquiry, and discussions, grades 6-12. New York: teacher College Press.*

McGough, A. (2023). A Clinical Psychologist who works with teenagers and adults and sits on the American Foundation for Suicide Prevention at North Carolina andis the chapter president.

Mervosh, S.(2024). A Crisis of School Absences. The New York Times.

NEA (2022). www.nea.org

NEA Ranking & Estimates Report (2023). teacher Pay & Per Student Spending

Nixon, A. (2024). Leeton School District to adopt four-day week. Warrensburg Star Journal

Rideout, N. (2022) Oregon Health and Science University American Academy of Child and Adolescent PsychiatrNews.ohsu.edu

PEW Research Center (2023). Schaeffer, K. 9 facts about bullying in the U.S. wwwpewresearch.org

PEW Research Center (2015). Sharrett, L. One-parent families in the U.S. wwwpewresearch.org

Posey, A. (2019). *ENGAGE THE BRAIN How to Design for Learning That Taps into the Power of Emotion.* Alexandria VA, USA : ASCD.

Putnam, R. (2001). *Bowling Alone: The Collapse and Revival of the American Community.* New York: Simon & Schuster.

Rideout, N. (2022). News.ohu.edu

Rhee, M. (1997). Founded The New teacher Project (TNTP), a leading organization in understanding and developing innovative solutions to the challenges of hiring new teachers.

Sanfelippo, J. (2023). superintendent for the Fall Creek School

District in West Central Wisconsin- In person.

Sauer, M. (2024). 42-year-old spent $1,000 to launch her Amazon side hustle-now it brings in $33,https://www.cnbc.com

Sharrett, L. (2020) *After 10 years of Hopes and Setbacks What Happened To the Common Core.* New York Times.

Schaeffer, K. (2023). 9 Facts about bullying in the U.S. www.pewresearch.org..

Scholastic and Bill and Melinda Gates Foundation (2010). *Primary Sources: America's teachers on America's Schools*. New York: Scholastic Inc.

Schwarz, J. E. (2005). "Realizing the American Dream: Historical Scorecard, Current Challenges,*Future Opportunities*" New York: W W Norton Company Inc.

Stickland, B. (1971). Manchester Bidwell Corporation. Provided market-driven career education created through strong partnerships with leading local industries.

Store.samhsa.gov

Sweeney, C. (2023). *Science Says Teens Need More Sleep. So Why Is It So Hard to Start School Later?* KFF Health News. Kffhealthnews.org

The Alliance for Excellent Education (1998). *How You Can Make a Difference* ww.wall4ed.org

Theobald, R. (2023). Deputy director of the Center for Analysis of Longitudinal Data in Education Research.

USAfacts.org

Wahlstrom, K. (2022). Education researcher for a National

Education Association

Walsh, J. A., and Sattes, B. D. (2015) *Questioning for Classroom Discussion Purposeful Speaking, Engaged Listening,Deep Thinking. Thousand Oakes, CA: Corwin.*

Weber, K. (2010). *"Waiting for Superman" How we can Save America's Failing Public Schools*. New York: Public Affairs

Weingarten, R. Has launched major efforts to place education reform and innovation high on the nation's agenda . Weingarten has been a history teacher and the president of the American Federation of Teachers (AFT).

www.gao.gov

www.schools.nyc.gov

Made in the USA
Middletown, DE
19 August 2024